RANTS AND RECIP.

RANTS & RECIPES

CHRIS BLAND

Happy reading,

Chris Bland.

SilverWood

Published in 2015 by the author
using SilverWood Books Empowered Publishing®

SilverWood Books Ltd
30 Queen Charlotte Street, Bristol, BS1 4HJ
www.silverwoodbooks.co.uk

ISBN 978-1-78132-337-3 (paperback)
ISBN 978-1-78132-338-0 (ebook)

British Library Cataloguing in Publication Data
A CIP catalogue record for this book is available from the British Library

Set in Sabon by SilverWood Books
Printed on responsibly sourced paper

This book is dedicated to small Gwen, a much loved and vital part of Acorn for many years and a wonderful mother.

To Alan for proofreading, Jen for typing it all and Hill for advice on publishing. Also, Blod, Sue and Marion, who have helped me over many years, actually at the 'coal-face'; to all the friends who have helped me out over the years; to all the young people who have worked for me; and to all those loyal customers who have enjoyed the food I have prepared.

Contents

Rants

Introduction

Well, here it is, the book that has been pending for years – at last! Customers and friends asked for recipes and advice. I gave out the occasional recipe but I was often too busy to provide them, or I made them up as I went along.

I often said, "You wouldn't read about it!" This will be in my book: folks won't believe these things happen. If James Herriot could write such an easy read about the veterinary profession, why couldn't I write a humorous rant about the mad world of catering to the general public? I once read a book about the adventures of a Norfolk café and thought, "Well, I can do better than that!"

My excuse had always been that I was too busy preparing all this food and I did want a life outside of it. There are only so many hours a day, and even with my amazing energy and capacity for work and play, there were limits. I had always been disciplined about finishing at 5 or 6pm. That was it for work! My days off were real days off! No business involvement at all. I think this is probably why I managed to go on for so long. You only have to look and see how short are the periods of time that people stick in catering, at the real coal face, in one outlet.

So when I went into semi-retirement, there really were no more excuses; it was now or never! If I left it until I retired totally I would never be able to sell it; whoever would want to buy it? Probably no one will anyway and I will have a lifetime's supply of ready presents for friends!

So, here goes, and it has to be called *Are You Still Open?* But wait, as I write – and rant – a better title is: *Rants and Recipes.*

Why Wholefood?

It would have been less controversial, a hell of a lot easier and I would have made far more money if I had done just normal café food. But it wasn't me to do 'ordinary' food! I couldn't back down on my passionate belief in wholefood and I probably hoped I could convert the nation – wrong, but I think I have shown a lot of people it's not just boring brown food, nuts, lentils and Jesus sandals!

Back in my late teens I was convinced by the wholefood message that natural was healthier. Using unrefined, low sugar, low fat, high roughage ingredients and second class protein (as it was called then) had to be better for our bodies and the planet. Food that is highly refined, high in calories and additives is surely not what our bodies were designed to assimilate. The fizzy, brightly coloured sugared drinks are surely not good for our body systems. Shouldn't food taste natural and not synthetic?

My beliefs were becoming a passion, and all of a sudden I was in a position to turn this into a commercial proposition and job for myself and my husband. Probably foolishly. I didn't realise how hard it would be. The vast ignorance about 'wholefood' – vegetarian, isn't it? Never mind being on a first floor and in the heart of serious meat-producing and meat-eating countryside!

I think you might agree with my thinking and actions when you look at Joe Public – seriously overweight, lacking in energy, colour and life force.

It seems to me that 75% of the population don't care what they eat – are ignorant of or choose to ignore the truth that 'You are what you eat'. They do not want to change their bad habits – just look into their supermarket trolleys at the food they buy and feed to their children. Just look at how Jamie Oliver got on!

Every day I am still amazed by the gross size of people. Officially, 63.8% of people in England are overweight. Just imagine carrying all those in bags of sugar on your body. No wonder they are lifeless. Even in our establishment, 25% of people who join us for a meal are overweight – seriously. Having climbed up our stairs, many are breathless, even the under 40s. Isn't it time we told these people that yes, they are fat? I'm told all this pussy-footing around with 'overweight' and 'carrying extra weight' doesn't work. But saying "You're fat" has miraculous effects and shocks people into serious action.

Slowly, slowly the government is realising that we have to do something. The UN have said that to prevent a massive cancer tidal wave, we must eat more unrefined food, fruit and vegetables. Also the massive rise in diabetes and all the extra health problems will stretch the NHS to breaking point – never mind heart disease and Alzheimer's, which are also food related to some degree.

Yet despite all this, every day I get people that won't enter the café because of 'wholefood'. Then when people do, it's a battle trying to explain things. No – I don't have chocolate cake, biscuits, mayonnaise or Coke. Am I dispirited? Downhearted? Yes, on many days, but my Sagittarius birth sign must buoy me up and not let me quit or get beaten down.

So I can soon leave my beloved baby, Acorn, knowing I tried to help the health of a nation – at least it kept me fantastically fit and active. I've always maintained I'll go down fighting, although the fight has been knocking me back over many, many years. Life will go on without Acorn – I shall stick to my wholefood beliefs. I will be totally frustrated and annoyed when I dine out. No wholemeal pasta or rice, no 'proper cakes' and too much sugar and salt in everything. As one famous lady said, 'This lady's not for turning'.

The real facts of wholefoods are:
1 Wholefoods are high in fibre and have a low GI rating. This means they don't promote sudden spikes in blood sugar levels. This keeps the insulin levels low, so less fat is stored and there's less hunger between meals.
2 The high fibre content and protective antioxidant properties of wholefoods reduce the risk of many

cancers – pancreatic, colon, breast, ovarian and uterine.
3   Wholefoods reduce high blood pressure, lower 'bad cholesterol' levels and raise 'good cholesterol' levels. This helps to reduce cardiac diseases and related problems.
4   They reduce the risk of developing type 2 diabetes and improve insulin sensitivity.
5   The fibre in wholefoods can benefit or prevent gastro intestinal problems. Even coeliacs can benefit from some wholefoods as they can reduce inflammatory reactions.
6   They are an effective way to control weight – the more whole grains you eat, the more weight you can lose. It is also an effective way to control weight in the long term. If you are interested in calories, the 'calorific density' of wholefoods is low.

So does anyone need any more reasons to eat a wholefood diet? I think I am a real life example of weight control through wholefoods. Many of my friends hate my size eight and ten clothes-shopping trips!

When I opened my doors twenty-eight years ago, this was the food I was passionate about, and still am – as friends know. In the 70s and 80s wholefood was in vogue and in my travels I saw lots of wholefood cafés successfully running in Wales. Sadly, very few are left, and with the folding up of Cranks in London, it seems there really is no hope. Recently, though, on an expedition to London, Kensington High Street, I saw that a large wholefoods store was operating. I was amazed and delighted. I need to relocate!

It is strange to think that many people said, years ago, that the organic movement would make things easier. It hasn't. With the recession of 2008–2014 came an abandonment of organic food and it is now only for the really dedicated and, I think, possibly more of a 'southern thing'. There are many people from the south who, over the years, have wanted me to relocate there, but never from the north.

Beginnings

Well, how did it all start twenty-eight years ago? An idea, a thought that had been fermenting over a period? I was a representative for a veterinary wholesaler, very successfully selling drugs and instruments. I was their first female rep and my area covered one sixth of the country. I have to say I loved the lifestyle and travelling. However the company started to change, changes I did not like. Promotion meant a job 'inside' and a possible move south that I didn't want.

At that time I was married to Ali, an Egyptian who lived in London. I lived a commuting lifestyle between Shrewsbury and London. Like most Egyptians, he wanted his own business, but we didn't think we were ever going to achieve this in London.

One day, on returning to my top floor flat in Sandford Avenue in Church Stretton, I found a note attached to the door. This note informed the general public that the present occupier of the first floor was vacating the premises. Cooking and the idea of a café had always been a passion for me, inherited from my paternal grandmother. Was this the opportunity that we were waiting for? My family owned the building and would be happy for a 'safe' tenant. Of course, we could fail and no rent would be paid! The idea was formed and quickly acted on. In a panic moment at Ludlow Council offices applying for change of use, 'Acorn Restaurant and Coffee Shop' was launched – on paper, anyway!

Three hard months of organising, furnishing, fitting kitchens and decorating followed. My father was a star in this, a fantastic 'handy man' and decorator. Ali moved up from London, I started baking, still doing my repping job part time. My mother supported Ali, preparing all the food. Ali was a natural charmer with the customers, though he wasn't quite so good in the kitchen and under pressure!

On 16 February 1986, the day we opened, I was working in Stoke on Trent. Yes, we did have customers in. Slowly, slowly it grew. We tried evening meals and special Egyptian evenings, and it all helped to pay the bills. By December 1986, we were going the right way. But I couldn't keep up two jobs, so I left my repping job for full time restaurant work.

Two years down the road, it wasn't working out. Two fiery temperaments, with one telling the other (me) how to cook! A tempestuous relationship ended in a traumatic divorce. I kept the Acorn and was responsible for everything. Ali opened a fruit and vegetable business down the road. After a few acrimonious months, when I closed down Acorn, we both continued our chosen professions.

I had a stalwart mother, 'small Gwen', who stepped back into preparing food, whilst I did front of house. Not my best position, but needs must!

Lots of lovely girls and a few guys have helped to man Acorn. Considering the number of years I've operated, I've had a very low staff turnover. They come and go, eventually, and they're generally lovely kids whose characters and hard work have helped to make Acorn.

A few other people have made up Acorn: Marion, Blod and Sue – who still helps me out. It's been a long road – probably too long, but all things come to pass.

This is a very short précis of all the years, hard work, heartbreak, changes, people and food that have passed through my doors. The main aim of the book is to record the hilarious, maddening and memorable people and events of the last twenty-eight years. I'll talk about events and people, my thoughts, my dislikes and likes, and especially comments customers have made.

I won't hold back on what I think about all sorts of issues that have affected the past twenty-eight years of Acorn life – maybe there will be a few rants, but then you would expect that from me anyway.

I also wish to record some of my many recipes that people have requested. It seems a terrible shame for all that knowledge to just disappear.

So here it is – recorded for posterity, or otherwise!

You Wouldn't Read About It!

Life at Acorn has never been short of incidents, laughter, head-banging and general incredulity at how unpredictable it all is. We can be totally empty, then have a horde of people appearing within the space of three minutes. Sod's Law! That's how we run! How else could our life be so entertaining and frustrating? What we sell out of on one day, no one will buy the next. Why is soup wanted even when it's twenty-five degrees outside? Why does nobody like cold soup in these temperatures? But when it is five degrees, everybody wants sandwiches and not one hot meat pie is sold.

Some incidents may amaze you, some may not even tick your box. Perhaps you've asked the question yourself:

"Have you a toilet?"

"Yes, thank you!"

It seems a strange British thing that people don't actually say what they mean.

"Have you got the milk?"

I have just carried two coffees, one in each hand, to a table of customers. I have not yet managed to grow a third hand! It would speed me up even more if I could.

"Have you any sweeteners?" always used to cause an intake of breath. Now I don't try to explain just how much more harm sweeteners can cause compared to sugar – although this was before the 'sugar is the new tobacco' movement got going.

We were once asked if the water from our hand wash basin was drinking water. Even Severn Trent provide us with decent tap drinking water!

How long does it take to decide what you want to drink? I suppose because I am such an instant person, I do find this unbelievable. Our menu does not offer ten types of coffee with twenty flavoured syrups, or every fizzy drink under the sun!

It must have been so much easier when it was tea, coffee, hot chocolate, lemonade, etc. Same old supermarket dilemma – give people too much choice and it's fatal.

"Can I have a nice cup of coffee?" is another request.

"No, we only do absolute rubbish ones." Requests for coffee provide much amusement at Acorn, as we do not possess an all-singing, all-dancing coffee machine. I have held out long and hard against the steaming, banging coffee machines that abound everywhere – I can't understand how they afford it. (However, I do a fantastic imitation of a hissing coffee machine.) We do the basics – filter, cafetière and good old-fashioned milky coffee, and not over-priced, flavourless, trendy coffee – if you can call it that! I have had a few people walk out because I do not provide cappuccino coffee. But they miss out on wonderful, flavoursome Machu Picchu coffee. Yes, you can survive without cappuccinos . If they only knew how many calories and rip offs they have encountered – frequently.

Then there is chocolate. What! No chocolate cake? Yes, we get people who can't survive without it. My nearest is chocolate and beetroot cake, and we do sell chocolate ice cream. We have had people walk out, obviously so addicted to chocolate that they cannot live for one day without their fix. Some parents are totally controlled by their chocolate-craving children. Cadbury's have done a wonderful job!

Cakes! Another topic that could fill a book. But I will just recall a few gems:

"Are these all the cakes you do?"

Only ten real homemade cakes to choose from! But no, they want lemon drizzle cake or Victoria Sandwich. What part of wholefoods do these come into? I have no idea! But sadly, I know, not many people actually understand what wholefood is. Or even notice the three inch high letters on my pavement signs and my entrance menus telling them this. Various other bizarre requests include sausage rolls and my personal pet hate – toasted teacakes. I've never seen a wholemeal one yet. M&S and Waitrose sometimes rise to wholemeal hot cross buns, which yes – we do serve on Good Friday!

I'm a great one for serving seasonal foods in our mass produced everything any time culture. I do the above and Simnel Cake at Easter. The explaining we have to do about that one. It is the 'mother of all cakes', though.

Mince pies and Christmas cake are served only at Christmas with, of course, mulled wine. Isn't it nice to have special things at special times? Not everything always – which, unfortunately, people seem to expect and don't appreciate. They don't even understand what seasonal produce is. The seasons have all merged into one, with air transport bringing in goods from all over the world all the time.

Wildly enthusiastic customers study the menu intensely for a few minutes and then order just two coffees. The menu is a source of much amusement. It is studied, but often there is little in the way of orders. It's all too much for them. The classic question is: "What's in the nut roast?" Funnily enough, nuts, and if I tell you all the other ingredients it will probably put you off totally, but actually it's very good and many people tell me so. They risk it, never having had nut roast before, then are amazed that they actually enjoy it!

This moves on to, "Do you do breakfast?" Yes, but not the sort you are after, methinks. The number of people who come in asking for cooked breakfasts! Yes, we do lovely porridge, muesli, toast, even beans on toast, but not the big fry-up! One beautiful sunny November morning, my first five customers trailed upstairs asking for cooked breakfasts. Only thirty metres away we have a place that can oblige – why me?

"Do you serve coffee?" beggars anyone's belief! And "You don't do cold drinks?" Well, on the menu there are at least six. "Do you do tea?" they ask after studying the menu and specials board for five minutes, I jest not. Then they order two teas – ordinary, of course!

The questions are beyond belief to a functioning, half intelligent human being! Why do people ask for things that are not on the menu? I know about the 'anything you want, madam, and just ask if you don't see what you want' brigade, but we sport nothing like this. We are trying to prepare seven cooked savoury dishes a day, plus all the on the spot sandwiches, potatoes, salads, etc., plus at least ten home-made cakes, fruit crumble and pies and another dessert when busy – plus scones! Is it any surprise I can be snappy and irritated by ridiculous questions? I defy anyone to cope with this all for twenty-eight years – and not become a jibbering heap!

Anyone who has dealt with the general public for years knows. Sometimes I'm amazed I'm still upright and have a sense of humour, a facet lacking in many customers who can't even say "hello" or "goodbye" and won't make eye contact. People really are extraordinary in their demands, questions, lack of humour and life-force, and inability to make a simple decision. We frequently say "How do they make important decisions when 'what would you like to drink?' produces silence?"

One day a woman came in with her son at 4.30pm-killing-after-school time, wanting chocolate cake then, of all things, ordered a date slice – they are sugar free and an acquired taste. On coming to pay she decided she was going to barter; after consuming three quarters of the date slice she was only paying £1.50 for that! I pointed out that this is not an eastern bazaar. A war of words ensued and I decided I never wanted her to darken my doors again! What an example for a youngster! How does one refrain from strangling these sorts of people? Answers in an email please!

Hidden Gems at the Top of the Stairs

On entering Acorn you are immediately confronted by a flight of sturdy banister-lined Victorian stairs with no immediate view of the café. It is definitely a psychological barrier for some people. There are those who won't even attempt the stairs. Yes, they are a deterrent, but also a filter system – just think what might come in off the streets. People open the door, look and walk away. Few are physically incapable of climbing them. In fact we have had blind people, people with cerebral palsy, one-legged, on crutches, with Zimmer frames, giant buggies and dogs, very, very old and young. It's attitude and guts! The worst non-climbers are obese women of forty plus. With the obesity epidemic, it will get worse – or funnier. I worry that my poor Victorian stairs will not be able to take the strain!

The stairs are our early warning system; when a door or a stair creaks, we know another challenge is on the way. Such fun!

Amazingly, a few times when I've left my flat gate open to the second floor, some people have walked through Acorn, up to the second floor and into the kitchen in my flat, and then asked, "Is this the restaurant?" If I had expected people to climb two flights of stairs to a café, I think I would have been in a dream world. (Although even I am amazed by some café locations, and their 'loo' trek has to be done to be believed.) Some people think I am so unique that they make comments such as "You are tucked away up here!" Obviously far more people use stair lifts and Costa-type cafés than I think.

We have many dogs that drag their owners off the street

and propel them at top speed up the stairs. Yes, the joys of a dog biscuit! Well at least someone appreciates us.

It is amazing the number of people who come in and say that they have followed this "delicious smell" down the street, making comments such as "That wonderful smell of garlic" and "What are you cooking? It smells wonderful in here!" Equally, we have had people who walk out because of the smell of garlic and spices – that awful smell of frying! There was even one comment: "I can't drink my coffee with that smell – garlic!"

Then there are the heads that appear around the door with a "Just having a look! Will be back!" I'm still waiting. Some climb the stairs, emerge into the room and say, "Isn't it lovely. What's that wonderful smell?" Then they retrace their footsteps all the way back down the stairs. It's not that bad! Just for a coffee. When I see the state of so many places in this country, I do wonder.

The comments and excuses I have heard are many and varied.

"Just looking, we'll be back for lunch."

"What time do you close?"

"Are you open tomorrow, Sunday, Christmas Day?"

One day two ladies appeared, read the menu and said, "Oh, yes. Lovely spiced yellow pea soup. No, we won't have a drink." I turned my back and they were gone.

One day a woman entered, interrogated the staff about everything from cakes to opening hours (perhaps she wanted to buy it?) then stared at the cakes and said she had never noticed the place before. "It's lovely," she said and then disappeared downstairs.

The number of people who come in, having "never noticed" it before. I've only had two pavement signs for twenty-eight years!

"How long have you been here?"

"Yes, I've been meaning to come in before."

Different folks with different attitudes. My friends and I would be looking for a place like Acorn – tucked away, not trendy or mass marketed. We must be good to have survived for twenty-eight years, tucked away upstairs with no direct street access – a hidden gem. (Acorn was actually, for many years, in a publication called *Hidden Gems*.)

I feel that for the next generation the situation will get worse, as they are so used to brand names and open trendy places, chromium palaces with piped 'musak'. Perhaps as they grow they will change: the number of people who have said, "Yes, it's just like my grandmother's!" or "Yes, the smells of my childhood."

Classics

Even now, the number of people who can't tell a crumble from a fruit pie leaves me speechless – they are of an age, surely, that they would have made pies and crumbles. Again, I must be presuming, as the people I know and move amongst have cooked or aspire to cook.

Take the two ladies who watched me stirring gooseberry jam and then asked, "Is it homemade?" at which Sue and I had to retreat into the kitchen.

The strange magic of homemade food is still a concept a lot of people really cannot understand, even with all the TV chef programmes. The fact that someone actually makes meat pies, fruit pies and crumbles, pizzas (this could go on for ever) starting from scratch with the basic ingredients, is beyond many people's comprehension. Certain things seem to be accepted, such as scones, cakes and quiches. Cakes, though, are another mine field. However, when we have gone through every ingredient, they do seem to understand.

In the early days I even cooked the baked beans and all the jam. But over the years, due to the pressure and non-appreciation, I now don't. After spending hours picking pricey and prickly gooseberries, topping and tailing them then boiling and bottling the jam, to be asked if we had strawberry jam…I throw in the towel!

I do still make some jam for 'special customers' and to give to friends when I visit. They really love it. I do still make the Shropshire dressing, marmalade, garlic butter and mincemeat. The list of everything else always amazes me, and yes, I wonder how I do it. Were it not for great organisational skills and deep freezes, we could not run the range we do. I keep meaning to cut back, but every time I suggest it, staff are in uproar about their special dish; and by offering a range of cakes I am trying to help the customers who stare in the cabinet, pull up their noses and say, "Are those the only ones you have?" On the other hand, one truly discerning customer once actually said, "I won't do you the discredit of asking for a toasted teacake in an establishment like this!" Eureka! Had I finally cracked it? I nearly kissed her. You cannot believe how a comment like this can make my day. This is the sort of person I always hoped I would be catering for – wrong!

Our 'milky coffee' still brings cries of "That was really lovely and tasted of coffee!" It is a drink of a certain generation. My mother, when she was alive, only liked that kind of coffee, and my aunties still do.

The café is awash with cuttings of latte, semi flat and white cappuccino jokes. I just want a coffee and empathise with people who are confused by all these names. We don't all want buckets of frothy, non-tasting coffee. A 'cup of coffee' is slowly becoming an extinct item, along with the teacup!

Bara Brith and tea bread when served as fruit cake seem to suffice. Flapjacks now seem acceptable for the more traditional and for children. Over the years I have tried so many cakes – what one person will rave over, another will find inedible, as in the case of date slices. The cake 'to die for' is my moist carrot cake, and so many people say it is the best carrot cake they have ever eaten. I would agree; I have given up eating it elsewhere as I am always disappointed. This recipe has been included in the cake section of this book, for all the people over the years who have marvelled at it. Now is your opportunity to make it for yourself.

It was quite difficult to choose which recipes to include in this book. Some stood out right away, but others I debated over. I didn't want to include recipes everyone does, but they are often the popular ones. My recipes always have a slight twist because of the wholefood aspect. Every cake and scone I bake has 100% stone ground organic flour. This fact is probably wasted on 75% of customers, but it makes it a little healthier. The sugar is always dark muscovado and reduced in quantity, eggs are free range and fats are top grade 100% vegan with no polyunsaturated and non hydrogenated fats. This fact people will never realise when they moan about the price of a piece of cake. Pastry and scones had to be included as people rave about these. They can't make either and their scones never rise. Mine have been known to cut into four slices; a record, I'm told by one adoring customer. My partner is always disappointed when eating scones out because a) they are never wholemeal, b) they fall apart and c) they are tasteless or stale. I often get asked if I have any "proper scones".

Strange Questions – Or is it Me?

"Is this the café?"

"Can we only have coffee?"

"Have you a toilet?"

"Where is the café?"

"Are you still open?" (This question was asked at 2.40pm.)

"What do you put in your nut roast?"

"Do you have water?"

"Can I have a nice coffee?"

"Is this the dog room?" (A sign on the door indicates this.)

"Where is the Tea Garden?"

"Do you do soup?"

"Have you any proper cakes?"

"Have you any gluten-free food?"

"Have you any ordinary scones?"

"Have you any gluten-free cakes?"

"Is the Tea Garden open?" (Mind you, the temperature is
    22 degrees, menus on every table.)

"Do you serve tea?"

Allergies and Dietary Requirements

Twenty-eight years ago the only allergy was to peanuts. Now, nearly every other person is intolerant to something. These people seem to be drawn to our café; because it is 'wholefood' and therefore its menu is sensitive to dietary requirements, people have noticed and are attracted by it. Their amazing ignorance about their allergies baffles me. I get asked for gluten-free, go through everything that is gluten-free and then they select a 100% wholemeal *wheat* cake. One of the many I have not recommended. I have now stopped questioning, reasoning or lecturing, I just answer their questions.

Once we had someone who was allergic to butter and ordered a jacket potato and butter, but didn't tell us that he was allergic to butter. I think if I was allergic to butter, that would be the first thing I would tell the waitress.

It does tend to be a game on the cake front – my ex-manageress retired screaming on this one. We recite a whole list of carefully constructed cakes; they don't really want one – it's a game: "We are trying to catch you out – we are special." Blod used to solve this by putting a gluten-free cake on a plate and serving it with "You asked for this!" which often produced the reply, "Yes, but we didn't really want it!"

The true coeliacs are eternally grateful they have a choice and are so shocked they find it difficult to choose. We can produce numerous products and we know what we are talking about. The other game is asking strange questions – asking if salad, jacket potatoes or ice cream are gluten-free! Have you ever eaten wheat-laden ice-cream?

There truly is a lot of misunderstanding regarding allergy, intolerance and the dreaded gluten and wheat. It does seem that wheat now is really affecting the gut and stomach of many people. This results in bloating and pain, so these people do want to avoid it. No problem with us. I have adapted lots of recipes to be wheat free. But after we've recited everything that's wheat free they then select the item that isn't!

Gluten intolerant people are so grateful and surprised that they have a choice – something I find amazing as it's so common now. Even the 'biggies' cater for it.

Once when we were with a party with a gluten-free diet person, the soup was OK (no big deal) but there was no gluten-free roll or rice cake to serve with it. This was a very prestigious catering outlet in Derbyshire trying to pander to an emerging market, but not really understanding the total concept of a gluten-free diet. If a small establishment in Church Stretton can get to grips with the situation, why can't a multi-chef, million-dollar establishment get it right?

Coeliacs, I'm told, don't tend to eat out too much as it is such a nightmare with staff and catering houses not understanding, making wild guesses or offering a bland "Don't know" ("Don't really care"). I can now vouch for this, having friends who are wheat intolerant and eating outlets that cannot provide the most basic oat cake, rice cake or cake.

This brings me on to vegans – another group we attract and cater for. Some days are better than others. But it's 'sod's law' that the day I cook a dairy soup, a vegan comes in. I try to avoid doing a dairy-based soup and vegetarian dish on the same day, as this would limit their choice drastically. I do have coping strategies for the broccoli or cauliflower and stilton soup now. It all comes with experience and cooking the product from scratch.

We can always offer something, and if I am around I can

guide people to cakes, puddings and main courses. They are very grateful we can provide dishes and know what we are talking about. A lovely group came in specially this January and were delighted and truly appreciative of the food we produced. It does make such a difference when we are serving people who are in tune with what we are doing. For whatever reason these people are vegan, they really care about what goes into their bodies. I won't get into the debate about the subject – but they seem to really understand the ethos of Acorn. Unfortunately for us, compared to the mass population they are a very small group.

I have a vegan couple (and baby!) who regularly ring up to check that I have a vegan soup on the menu for that day and travel many miles for this 'treat'. They also have the delights of a vegan fruit crumble with Swedish glace or soya cream.

The general ignorance about wholefood and vegetarians results in most people from Church Stretton thinking that we are a vegetarian café: it's always been so. Yet, surprisingly, after soup, meat pies are our best seller, and we have even had comments from customers saying that there is too much meat in them! Yet I received an email recently complimenting me on the quantity of meat in my meat pie!

Vegetarian food is a bit of a nightmare. I love cooking it – it provides a challenge and I can use my creativity. It is one of my many interests although I am not vegetarian. However, there are challenging issues. Tofu, Quorn and beans don't sell very well to Mr Average. If we do pasta and broccoli gratin everyone loves it – but here's the problem, vegans don't! Anything with cheese will sell, apart from to the groups we are trying to cater for.

Spicy food – again, it's a nightmare. We don't get the Vindaloo set, but as with anything spicy we're always asked, "How hot is it?" I don't do hot as I seem to be intolerant to chilli – but spicy, yes. I love my Eastern spices, and having been married to an Egyptian, I was introduced to and developed a love for spices and foods that I had never before encountered.

Vegetarian food consumption is very varied. Many people, like myself, eat veggie foods but aren't wholly vegan or vegetarian. We get days when we sell hardly any vegetarian or vegan dishes and days when they are a sell-out. People can be very conservative about food – perhaps anything too different freaks them. Possibly it's because people are paying money and they want to know they'll enjoy it. The picking out of olives and even peppers still goes on – and garlic phobia.

When we started, we were serving pitta bread, olives, hummus and feta cheese before most of Shropshire had heard of it. Now it's old guard even in the most remote pub to find olives for nibbles. I've stopped doing it now the rest of the world has caught up.

Good and Bad Moments

We have had plenty of those over the years. I have rejoiced in some, risen above others, banged my head and kept breathing on other occasions. When you are at the coal face with the general public for eight hours a day, five days a week for twenty-eight years, you put up with a lot. Your nerves are stretched to breaking point – your tongue lets rip sometimes and you laugh a lot. I have never yet been reduced to tears in front of the public. In my personal life, I have had a lot of heart-break, stress and incredible pressure. I have also had a lot of fun, laughter and adventure – just a typical life, really.

I'm including a small selection of incidents from over the last couple of years, since note-taking started. They might surprise, they might shock, they might bore you a bit but at the time they were significant.

On one occasion, two coffees were served in the Tea Garden. On delivering them we discovered children drinking from other soft drink company products, bottles of water and take-away coffee from a rival establishment. Then they asked for a refill for their bottle. People have used our Tea Garden, even our café, as a place to eat other people's ice-creams and ice-lollies, literally eating them in front of us!

One amazing incident: I looked out of the storeroom window one day to check the Tea Garden and spied a couple eating their own sandwiches and drinks on my Tea Garden tables. They seemed surprised when I requested that they leave immediately.

We have had smokers out there – despite being a 'healthy café' with 'No Smoking' signs displayed and no ash trays. We have also found cigarette ends and even dog poo deposited in the Tea Garden. I even caught two people with a dog, walking in off the street to use our Tea Garden as a dog toilet.

Yes, you wouldn't read about it.

On many occasions, when I have been gardening in the Tea Garden, potential customers have wandered in, looked around, sometimes responded when I acknowledged them, and then disappeared before my staff could take an order. Or they come up from the Tea Garden, ask questions, we tell them the daily specials and they then go back to relate the information to their group. We send down staff to get their order. But, hey presto, they have disappeared. The worst thing by far was preparing four meals, only to find when taking them down that the people had disappeared. Yes, this has now resulted in customers ordering and paying at the counter upstairs. It is strange how some people are hostile to paying before they have received their food.

People have sometimes read the menu for five minutes and then asked, "Do you do egg on toast?" Well, I don't see it on the menu! The strange requests for items not on a menu – particularly as there are two menus on display before you get to the counter as well as on the tables. Everything is carefully listed on the menu with reference to a blackboard for daily specials and with prices. Why is it so baffling?

We do occasionally get told that the soup is not hot enough – but one of my personal favourites was to be told that the soup was too hot.

There are people who come in for a coffee and "only have ten minutes". We could have served a meal in that time. Also there are those who come in for a meal but only have half an hour. Again we could serve three courses in that time – depending on your speed of eating. Buses to catch – train – no pressure, what!

What happened to manners? No wonder we have to write books about them – re-teaching people. When did thank you or please go out of fashion?

The rudeness and intrusion of mobile phones seems to upset a lot of people, including myself. I didn't want to put up yet another notice, requesting people to speak quietly or even banning them. It is the intrusiveness and the loud, silly ring tones. We do not want to know everyone else's business. I have had serious bank and solicitor's conversations go on at top volume in the café. Very important to them, but not to everyone else. The phone is always answered at top volume on loud speaker. Rarely do people leave the room to continue their conversation in private.

The land line telephone is another source of annoyance. I used to run the length of the building to answer it. It was inevitably someone trying to sell me something or change energy suppliers. So I stopped responding. I'm amazed at the amount of people who ring a café at lunch time then wonder why I have no time to speak to them. What a dreadful job these poor call centre people have – but we are all trying to do our job.

Cups, saucers and spoons do seem to have become surplus to most people's requirements. Things are put directly down on tables. The confusion over mugs and cups now astounds me. When did we forget what a tea-cup or mug was? I fear we have Starbucks to blame for this. Not serving saucers baffles me. What do you do with teaspoons?

Loud sucking of soup and coffee is not an inducement to everyone else to enjoy a peaceful cup of coffee. Children are strictly assessed before straws are given out to try and avoid the blowing of sticky drinks all over the table.

Sometimes it's hard to get a grunt as we give our cheery hello or goodbye and thank you. Some we like by their coming and some by their going.

We have had a man in with skis, a man dressed as Batman,

an Elvis look-alike and a man wearing a leather dog collar – it must have hurt as he coughed for most of the visit.

We have had people who wouldn't make eye contact, had dreadful anxiety problems, anorexia, controlling mothers, fathers and husbands – a few wives as well. It's usually the husband who is pleasant, smiles and says hello. We often wonder how they put up with some of the wives. There are also the wives who speak for their husbands and decide what he is going to eat, and definitely no garlic.

It's amazing how many 'domestics' we have observed, with raised voices and tears. One memorable couple had been having a very fraught lunch, and when they were leaving one of my youngsters said "Have a nice day!" We just went into hysterics.

There was the incident when a gentleman stated he couldn't eat wholemeal toast then ordered it and ate it. His harassed wife said, "Well, you're eating it now!" She took the words completely out of my mouth – one up to her. She had pandered to him for years. Perhaps we had had a mini wholemeal breakthrough.

The sign on my door clearly states that we are open on Saturday, Sunday, Monday and all school holidays. I was in the building one Tuesday when the doorbell rang; I opened it as I thought it was the postman.

"Are you open?" they enquired.

"Well, what does the sign say?"

"Oh, I thought it was Monday."

If we wanted someone to come in off the street, through a closed gate, a sign-blocked path and a closed and locked door with a sign saying 'Closed', they wouldn't do it. It is amazing, though; when the gate is shut and the door is shut, people still come up the stairs.

Many times, a customer has said "I'll have a coke!" My reply "Oh no you won't!" brings total incomprehension to some. I spent ten minutes one quiet afternoon explaining to one baffled customer the dreadful and harmful ingredients in this product.

I think I may have made one convert. I've stuck to my guns and never allowed any such rubbish or supported the giants of Coca Cola over the lifetime of Acorn, and I have survived!

Our 'no mayonnaise' policy baffles most people. The high calorific and mass-produced substance is a non-starter. I personally hate it and have a clear phobia after making, or trying to make, endless batches for A-level Home Economics.

Toilet Sagas

Yes, a very strange subject to write a chapter on, but possibly one of the most annoying and funny subjects connected to Acorn.

"Do you have a toilet?" quite a number of people have asked while staring at a large sign four inches high and fourteen inches long, printed in bold black letters: TOILET. Yes, we do, thank you, and we also have hot and cold running water.

Over the years people have repeatedly raced up our stairs and into the toilet. This baffles me as they are people who don't know the place, and yet are into the loo like whippets. As I didn't open a public toilet, I really do object to this – they don't ask, just use. As I have to pay for every drop of water, loo paper, soap and cleaning I really do see red, so I placed a notice on the door saying that as a customer you can use the toilet, but if not, a donation of 50p for the Severn Hospice would be appreciated. We must get a lot of donations as Severn Hospice is always amazed at how much my box collects, well above anywhere else in Stretton. We are their star establishment.

I have razor sharp eyes and ears – yes, still! My game of 'shame the cheats' has produced some comic comments, lies and deceit. "I have no change", "The wife's on the pavement downstairs", "I didn't know you had to pay", "I'll just go and get some change". Yes, I've even followed people into the street for their change! I think it's a fair enough deal, and the number of real customers who give a donation is astounding. I do think people don't seem to understand the plain English: "Customers free. Non-customers, a donation please."

The crafty way some sneak in, hover washing their hands, then when they think no one is about, race up the corridor to try and beat the 'Vigilante Bland'! They have been known to come with the whole family, and of course it's always 'the child' that urgently needs the toilet. No problem – just cough up. The other classic is to ask to use the toilet and say they are coming back later. I need not say – they never do.

It's much harder to police when the Tea Garden is open, as I have no idea of the customers and my staff seem clueless when asked. Yes, I have had to apologise a few times!

The other strange phenomenon is ex-customers coming back one hour, three hours or even half a day later and just rushing to the toilet. No "Hello, can I use your toilet again? We were customers" or "Thank you". There's now't so queer as folk! Another ploy is a couple will sit down and study the menu while one goes to the toilet. When that person returns, the other one goes, then returns. On trying to obtain an order, at least twice, we are told that no, they are not staying, and they depart, having emptied their bladders!

My toilet is a source of great amusement as it has the tank above and a long chain with a handle on – or it did. The ancient wooden very plain handle was stolen about four years ago – yes, you may find that as incredible as I did. It had been there for twenty-four years and must have been nicely germ-ridden. The garish replacement was not removed till someone, in sympathy, bought one more in keeping with our loo. Three months on, it's still there. We do have children who are really baffled, as they have never seen a loo chain before and think that they cannot flush the toilet. Of course some reminisce about "Mum's" or "Granny's" loo – someone even wanted to buy it off me. Children have been known to go down and use it at least twice, in utter fascination.

I have had loo rolls stolen and disgusting things put in the bin. Again, because I have a 'thing' about toilet hygiene,

I am always checking it to remove the various substances people deposit on the floor – the worst was vomit!

One of the best accolades I received was when a retired hygiene inspector used my toilet and declared that it was one of the cleanest he had been to in many, many years. I never cease to be amazed how dirty and unloved so many loos are – even in tiny tea-shops. The staff are lolling at the counter when it would just take ten minutes with a cloth and bleach to wipe over pipes and walls. Yes, toilets don't come much older than mine, but the pipes and skirting board are regularly wiped over. I think that if the loo, that people see, is like that, what is the kitchen, that people don't see, like? Our kitchen is open for the customers to see and marvel at what comes out of such a small space.

Two folks came in one day. One ordered a meal, the other nothing at all. They used our loo for at least ten minutes (oh dear) and then proceeded to sit for another half an hour, still having ordered nothing. Eventually they left, having spent the grand sum of £7.50. Then, such was the state of the loo, we spent the next five minutes doing a total cleaning job. One of my senior staff completely lost it. These things really irk one.

And finally...what part of 'wash your hands' after using the toilet don't people understand? It seems men are not the only culprits and it is amazing how many people don't do this last act. This was one of Blod's 'red mist' triggers.

The Tea Garden

This is another area of amusement and bafflement when people come upstairs into the café, having passed 'Tea Garden' signs on the way, and then ask which way to the Tea Garden. Obviously roof top gardens must be the vogue in areas of England.

The number of people who walk in and out when I am down there gardening and say, "Just looking" amazes me! Do they want bouncy castles, clinical matching chairs and tables? Not just the oasis of peace and calm, plants and birds that I have created.

Others, of course, love it at first glance, watching my sparrows in the bird bath and amongst the trees. They love the smells and the peace and quiet, and admire the various shrubs that make a bid for sunlight.

The system we have now adopted is: order at the counter, pay and then we supply. Works much better than before – good old Blod! Although it does get a bit hairy when people queue at the counter to give orders and block everything up. Most people seem to accept paying up front now. We don't get the walking off after food was ordered and finding no-one to deliver the food to.

Of course, in good weather everyone wants to sit out there. The café is empty and we turn people away. Equally, when it is very hot, it is a sun trap and people retreat to the coolness upstairs. Consumption of food really decreases in hot weather – yet European countries don't seem to suffer this with Brits on holiday. Our consumption of scones, however, does increase then, but usually without the cream. One searing hot day – 28 degrees – all we served were scones or drinks. People also seem to find it more difficult to make decisions as the temperature rises. We have had many tables ordering one tea and scone between two! At lunchtime of course!

It is strange how people let their dogs roam off lead, getting in the way of waitresses and other customers. Some dogs even set up territorial rights, and the owners have to be asked to keep them quiet and in check. Most dog-owners are eternally grateful that we take dogs in the garden – but dogs are another chapter!

I have had children jumping up and down on top of Tea Garden tables while consuming their own food and drink! They bring someone else's ice-creams in to eat. We have even had people, who are not customers, parking their bikes in the Tea Garden, then going off and eating in other establishments!

We have had plants stolen, plaques, even an umbrella – although I think that may have been carried out by boisterous local youths one Saturday night! The Tea Garden did have access 24/7 most of the time. I went through a gate locking stage, but it got too complicated. Now it's Fort Knox, but it won't stop the theft of sugar bowls, salt cellars and plants.

One of the most incredible incidents was a disappearing table! On unlocking the gate to the Tea Garden and entering it, I noticed one of my tables had disappeared! Trying to get my thoughts together as to where it could possibly be, I had a eureka moment about the refurbishing of the shop below me. On going to look through their window, I saw my table, covered in dust and being used as a saw bench! This was rather a problem as it was a Bank Holiday weekend with no workers likely to appear, yet it was urgently needed in the Tea Garden! A phone call to the future occupiers resulted in eventually, at 4pm that day, their arrival to rescue and clean-up my blemished table! There were profuse apologies regarding the cheek of their conduct and promises of a replacement table! All part of the challenge of Bank Holidays!

Ah – but the new trendy name for a tea garden is garden patio area.

Dogs and Children

A notice at the bottom of the stairs says it all: 'Dogs welcome and well-behaved children.' Yes, I make no excuses here. I chose not to have children and I don't want other people's badly-behaved ones. Fortunately wholefood doesn't tend to attract children, but some do slip in – even babies. I've always been worried about the amount of things people leave behind. Someday, possibly, we may find a baby in the garden!

I'm sure that everyone knows that kids now rule. Everything they say or do must be fawned over. They can't sit down, sit still, be quiet or say thank you. Eating choices are entirely dictated by the child, even though the adults may be craving for a nut roast. Tough luck, Mum!

Every parent seems to think their children are 'well behaved'. We are used to hearing threats.

"You saw the sign!"

Can't they control their own kids? You will all be aware of kids running everywhere, noisy, opening things and generally annoying other customers. So the owner has to step in as the parents seem to have no control over their offspring.

"Don't open that door!" (Even though the sign says 'staff only').

We have to try and stop kids running into staff carrying food, jumping down the stairs near the loo, while the parents think everyone wants to hear Little Johnny's gems or screams.

Their favourite party trick is licking their finger and putting it into the sugar bowl, then repeating the process – many times! I have been known to bag the sugar up for parents and charge them for it. The policy now is to remove all the sugar bowls if kids are at the table. Of course, the parents say, "They never do this at home!"

Perhaps no one has sugar bowls now or they are deprived of them – highly unlikely in a sugar addicted era, I feel. I've also watched with horror children drinking straight from a milk jug – with Granny, Mummy or Auntie looking on – but then the age of the milk jug has passed in favour of the plastic carton.

Usually, we hear them from afar – loud noises, bang, crash as they come through the doors, racing to a table which they eventually choose. Having let them study the menu, all of six years old, the parents allow them to order. As if they are likely to eat any of it! I know it would be sensible for them to order cheese jacket potato or sandwich, these being two of the items children are most likely to eat – despite the subsequent damage to the floor – instead of waiting ten minutes for them to dissect the menu, then choose an item that they will pick over and leave. They are then allowed to order an ice cream.

I'm still amazed at the children coming in at 10.30am who are allowed to eat ice-cream. Ye gods! This was a Sunday afternoon treat in another era.

The presentation of food to a child requires the magic words "Thank you". Of course, they always say this at home! I was even asked by one mother if I could come and teach her children table manners, to which I had to reply that either the child wouldn't last five minutes or would become a reformed character under my tutelage.

One precocious child dragged his uncle in, as he had done to every other establishment in Church Stretton, because he wanted to try us. We seemed to reach the small child's standard, although I still await his return with parents. At least he was well behaved.

Amazingly, we do provide high chairs, a thing that parents seemed surprised by. But most children won't sit in them. Even supplying children's books to try and keep them amused does not work. Not a lot of use in this electronic age. At least mobile phones keep adolescents amused.

We have had a few amazingly well behaved, charming children. They know the rules. Two lovely children so enjoyed the hot pork pie, the ice-cream and the ambience, they wanted to spend Christmas Day with us! Some even say "thank you" and quietly enjoy our books and our food.

The mess children can make is beyond belief, and the extra work it takes for one of the staff to clean the table and floor is probably not even thought of. A few kind parents have volunteered to brush up the mess. The joys of ground-in cheese on the carpet! It takes some specialised treatment and we do need the time before the next influx of feet. It really is incredible and has to be seen to be believed.

It amazes me that children don't seem to have been challenged or restrained from an early age. If I say "No" or give 'The Look', I mean it. I rarely get any cheek back or have a request refused. Are parents just worn down? Answers on a postcard please!

Another incident that I have seen, possibly twice, is the baby's nappy being changed on top of the restaurant table! No mat! A lovely combination for the tables that you eat off. Fortunately we spotted it and were able to disinfect. Most mothers ask for changing facilities and we willingly offer the office. Our loo is a bit cramped for such activities, but I have noticed that it has been done!

One toddler lay down on the floor, on his back, screaming and kicking to such an effect that my adjoining neighbour raced around, thinking that I was being attacked. The father eventually realised that this was not acceptable behaviour and removed the child.

Now let's talk about debateable subject of allowing dogs in Acorn.

We can do it because we have two separate rooms. As a one-time avid dog owner but now eight years 'dog-less', I can see both sides of the argument. We do have a 'dog friendly' room which is greatly appreciated, but is it too much to ask to have normal sized dogs, no more than two, clean and well behaved? Give people an inch and they take a mile. I know so many lovely dogs and owners, but we do get the 'freaks'. Irish Wolfhounds in a café? They occupied the whole room and smelt. Two or three huge breeds with one owner! Or the girl who had two collies and a baby and took over the whole room until asked to let other customers occupy the room. I'm still incredulous that people would want to bring two or three huge, hairy dogs into a café while they have coffee. Yappy and barking – some have had to be asked to remove their dogs; no serious fights yet, but a few 'nearlys'. We frequently have two or three separate lots in room 2. One memorable day I even had to let them spill over into the office.

My regular dogs drag their owners in off the street for their biscuit. We have had so many characters – Kinny, Milly, Tally, Boot and Charlie. Nearly always far better behaved than children. It's always the owner's fault if there is a problem. I did nearly faint when a woman came up saying, "I see you take dogs, but I don't suppose you will take seven?"

Amazingly, some tuck under tables and we would never know they were there. Other owners let their dogs sprawl all over the room, completely blocking it for serving. Just step over my dog with hot soup! Please.

The obesity among dogs now compares with owners. We've had one Rhodesian ridgeback who weighed more than I did, a fat whippet on spindly legs that barely held it up, a three-legged dog, blind ones and puppies in their first café, socialising, resulting in a wet carpet. The staff are sometimes is ecstasy over a "cute puppy" or a "Heinz 57" variety, sometimes horrified by the hairy, angry, ugly, smelly ones. Fortunately, only a few of my staff haven't been dog-friendly, and those that aren't are usually so because of lack of previous contact. They have all been child-friendly, though, as someone has to protect me from them, and vice versa.

We seem to specialise with guide dog training and also blind people with their amazing guide dogs. We are not allowed to give them biscuits because of their strict diet. But a friendly pat seems to suffice!

We have had a dog bowl stolen from the garden and one left there. We have had requests for a tea for a dog in the garden. One obese creature was even ordered an ice-cream, an unusual part of the canine diet, not recommended by vets!

Soon we'll see dogs too obese to get up the stairs – it's already happening with the general public!

Incidents

One of the funniest incidents that Blod recalls was when three females came in rather strangely dressed – but nothing new there. After having quite a jolly chat, one went to the loo. When we asked to take their order one said, "Can we wait? He's just gone to the loo." Well, evidently my face was a picture! We spent most of the next half an hour trying not to stare and cracking up in the kitchen. There have been many incidents of a similar nature over the years when we have had to retreat into the kitchen to 'get a grip'. One of my classic faux pas was on serving a gay guy a flapjack, I asked the standard question – "Plain or fruity?" He didn't bat an eyelid but I dissolved in the kitchen.

The woman with the knitted doll pinned on her jacket also had the girls in hysterics. Then there were two bikers with racoons' heads and tails on their helmets.

When the numerous Lycra clad cyclists come in, it's hard to avert our eyes. Really! Some should never attempt Lycra. I was once given a card, 'Don't do Lycra after 50!' but it does depend on the figure. The click, click of studs warns us that we are about to be invaded by fifteen or more sweaty, raucous cyclists leaving their precious £2,000-plus bicycles to take over the Tea Garden. Well, they are a breed unto themselves, as any true cyclist will admit. We have had some charming ones and some very, very noisy ones. Some were so bad that I had to go in and tell them to moderate their language and the volume. It is rather unnerving to any other customer trying to enter – although I do herd cycling groups into Room 2. The meanness of them and the strange food and drink that they request – decidedly not healthy – have always amused me. We try to convert them to some healthy food, more in keeping with their hobby.

A young Japanese lady once moved in for two and a half hours. She was on her computer, then her mobile phone for three quarters of an hour in high pitched Japanese – fortunately we were empty. One bowl of soup and a cup of coffee later, she reloaded her backpack and departed. A Japanese family discovered us and returned two days running from north Shropshire, they were so over the moon with our healthy selections. Another Japanese lady bravely tried my 'Italian Tofu' as she had never thought to cook it like that. She was amazed and thought it was wonderful. This has possibly now been reproduced in Japan!

A lovely Kiwi family were so enamoured with our food they declared that it was the best so far on their trip. Even the youngsters thought it was delicious. I've always thought that New Zealand was way ahead of us in the healthy eating stakes – Maoris aside!

A young couple, one winter afternoon, was so delighted that I was still serving food at 3.30pm as they had specially detoured after reading about us. They were overjoyed with my soup, garlic bread and speciality teas and the fact that we did 'real' coffee in cafetières.

Perhaps the funniest incident, after the initial shock, was when staff found a plate of false teeth on the table – and these were never reclaimed.

Good incidents like this really do make it all worthwhile!

Sponsored Trek and Cycle

In February 1999 I was probably at my lowest ever ebb after the death of my dear sister Jill from breast cancer the previous December. One day a Macmillan Newsletter dropped through my letterbox. On reading the contents, I found that a sponsored Sahara Trek near the Atlas Mountains in Morocco was being organised in the December of that year. They were appealing for challengers and the date that it finished was the anniversary of Jill's death. I felt that this was meant to be. I mulled it over for a few weeks and decided I would do it, even if it meant using my own funds. We had to raise a certain sum before we actually raised any sponsorship money.

I composed a letter, a friend printed loads of copies for me and I began sending them to all my friends and acquaintances. I put a board at the top of Acorn's stairs with photos, an explanation letter and sponsorship forms in the café. Hey presto!

It became my focus for ten months. I walked regularly with dogs, and up and down my stairs, so fitness was not a problem. Luckily it was a hot summer and I would try and walk at midday, when I could get away from the café. A friend kindly gave me the use of her caravan in Borth, so on my two days off I would drive over, stay overnight and walk up and down the sand dunes with my dogs. Inevitably, my one deranged dog, Molly, used to run off and disappear. So I spent further time racing around tussocks in the sand dunes, hunting for said dog. I attribute my super fitness to chasing after that dog.

I was worried about heat and blisters, never having had

walking boots till then. I acquired a pair of 'second-foot' leather ones, broke them in to my feet and never got a blister. The surgical spirit daily may have helped, and 'no-blister socks'. Whatever, it worked.

The reason for including this episode in the book is that the café was so fantastic for getting sponsors. I never presented my sponsor form to anyone I did not know and just left it on the table. Money was up front and it was a licence to print money, people were so generous. This was in the early days of the sponsored challenges and it was a novelty still. Only one person declined to sponsor me, saying he didn't understand the 'gist' of it! But later, he gave a donation.

Friends helped with various events and money flowed in, but it was mainly through direct sponsorship that I raised over £6,000 for Macmillan funding.

Needless to say I did the walk and felt a bit of a fraud as I found it so easy, even in the heat. It actually rained. I usually walked wearing two layers. I kept a diary and did a photo album for the café. Years after, people still find it interesting. I still have it, to relive what seems a lifetime ago. I made some really good friends out there through this walk.

So on to the next 'challenge'. For my fiftieth birthday I took up cycling again. Seeing so many fit and fanatical cyclists, I thought I should try it. It was a necessity when I was a school kid in Church Stretton, so why not try again?

My first foolish trip up hill and down dale resulted in me ending up on the Corvedale B4368 at Diddlebury – eleven miles away. I never thought that I would get back, but I did, though my legs were like jelly. Anyway I must have got hooked and was regularly off on my bike.

Hey presto! Another Macmillan Newsletter, and I discovered that they were organising a cycle challenge in South Africa, 600km along the Garden route – the Plettenburg Way. I had to raise minimum sponsorship again – but this was another 'meant to be' moment. This really was going to be the last one, I reassured sponsoring friends and customers. I had been so heartened by the real interest and generosity of everyone on the first one, I thought we could stand one more, and I was right. Same model sponsor form at Acorn and the pounds flowed in again. We did a few events to boost things and – hey presto – £6,000 plus again, and I paid my own expenses. At this stage 'sponsored events' were just getting the bad reputation of being a paid holiday.

Well, if you are in any doubt about this, let me tell you from the horse's mouth – this was the hardest, toughest thing I have ever done. Long, long days in the saddle, the dust, pitching tents after I had cycled 100km on hard ground was no joke.

On the first night of the most amazing 'off road' I had ever done, I thought it was all over – cold, shaking, unable to eat, desolate, I turned in.

The next morning, with the fantastic team spirit and camaraderie, I sprang into the saddle of my bike and was off. The off roads were the worst as I hadn't trained or ever done any serious off road before – but I did it! 60km in gale force wind (the equivalent of 125 miles, I was told!) was my epiphany moment. If not for team spirit and 'slip stream' I might not have made it. I was so late in, someone even took pity and pitched my tent for me. It was reported my bike was minus loads of gears – but I never got a puncture, though there were a few chain incidents!

Yes, it really was and still is the toughest thing I have ever done. Even Triglav – Slovenia's highest mountain – Snowdon, the West Highland Way or the Milford Track were nothing in comparison to that.

It was the terrain, heat and dust, day after day in the saddle. Not to make too much of a drama of it, we were the guinea pigs for this route, and since then it has been modified. So this time I certainly felt that I had earned my sponsorship. Again, I had kept a diary of photos. So another album graced Acorn to show to my generous supporters as they appeared over the year. The grand total was £7,072.50.

As I arrived back early, I took an earlier train and was nearly thrown off it as I should not have been on that train. However a compassionate conductor took pity on me, probably because when Blod met me she said that I looked like something from Biafra. She had madly agreed to man Acorn while I was away. Amazingly, this stint did not put her off coming to work a four year stint as manageress later.

Staffing

This is another chapter about great companionship and help, things I had not been used to since Gwen's day. A one-woman business can be lonely, hard and soul destroying, slogging away and having to cope with everything on your own. The silly incidents you laugh over, crazy people you deal with and pressure of work are all easier when shared with a kindred spirit, someone with empathy when you face endless shopping, storing, producing and trying to keep everyone happy and busy.

In 2007 we really upped the pace in marketing and custom. To enable us to do this I had to take on another full time Wonder Woman, and this was Blod. This was four years before the recession kicked in. We look back now at the sheer volume of work we got through and the pace at which we did it. As Mae West said, to get a job well done, "give it to two old broads".

The ups and downs of casual staffing would fill a book in itself. I have been very lucky with the girls and boys we have attracted. They either don't fit in during the first few months and go, or they stay for years. We sometimes employ whole families of brothers and sisters – at least five families have graduated through the Acorn café.

They are hard work at first – common sense isn't common. Why use three plates when they can use one? Or dirty the work surface and not clean up as they go along? What don't they understand about replacing a lid on a jar and putting it back where it came from? Poor Sue goes incandescent about this. Another of their 'party tricks' is to take a tea towel and abandon it on the counter. Worse still, they encase inside the tea towel a teacup, or an assortment of cutlery which then crashes, quite spectacularly, over the kitchen floor when the tea towel is rescued. It's one of the many things I've got used to.

The young staff really do find it difficult to gauge the correct time to go out and ask for an order. Don't ignore, don't rush but do make eye contact, we tell them. We now try and get them to get a drink order first as this splits the workload. It also gives everyone more space and people feel that they are being dealt with and not ignored.

We do have to start with the basics when we get them first. They'll ask "What things do they need for soup?" (The cutlery is a soup spoon and knife – difficult with a fork.) Here we go with families not sitting down to proper meals. We have them put all cups and mugs on saucers and always use teaspoons.

Don't put your fingers in cups, soup bowls, glasses and dessert bowls. Wash your hands. Remove old plates and dishes before you serve anything else. But don't snatch cups and teapots away – unless it's 5.15pm!

Don't take orders on trays to tables where customers kindly help unload them and then it all overbalances – this is usually learnt from experience as they don't listen to my advice. The same advice goes for putting a loaded tray anywhere near where a baby is stationed, as a hot cup or food is always grabbed.

Don't pretend that you don't know the size of a slice of cake or a portion size of crumble after two years! Sometimes the huge portions amaze me, and other times I am horrified by the small size.

It's been uplifting to see so many come to us unsure, quiet and hesitant, and develop into self-confident, quick and alert youngsters. With some young staff I seem to have more empathy and vice versa. Some I could have shaken or banged my head at their ignorance and slowness. Many have kept in touch and are now producing offspring of their own. Some write, some visit when 'back home'. I don't do Twitter or Facebook so no contact there – good old fashioned personal relationships. Many have achieved all sorts of things in their varied chosen professions. Of course, no-one has gone into catering. They have seen the real side of it. They do all seem to realise the constant hard work it all involves. It is amazing how very little some youngsters want 'to do work' now – or certainly the physical side of things. We hope we are instilling some kind of work ethic into them, although I do feel I have failed with some. Very few, as yet, have gone on to self-employment, but with a lot of folks that comes later in life. Many trips and countries abroad have been visited and worked in – on some of their hard earned wages. Often the entry at thirteen to Acorn has resulted in ten years' employment, coming back from college and university to do a few shifts. It has even been used in between jobs and various university degree courses.

I have never really had any major personality clashes. They eventually seem to realise who is boss and pays the wages. I have had a few battles, but eventually won. Honesty and reliability has usually been very good. I can't and won't put up with unreliability; it lets the whole team down and puts extra pressure on other people – always giving me more work and stress. We have to open and cope, come what may.

Of course, over the years I have had many staff crises, such as mixed-up shifts when two arrive for one shift and no one for another. Staff sickness or some family event making work impossible puts tremendous pressure on me and others. It's amazing how we always cope, even on walkers' Sundays, bank holidays and Easter holidays. Some days, yes, the air gets blue, plates are slammed. It's hard trying to deal with the general public, produce food and clear up. 'Wonder Woman', as I am known, does do miracles and works at twice the speed of most people. This is probably why I am still in business. I have an ability to react to the situation and gear up. We don't have a dish-washer. I've always maintained I can do it more quickly than loading and unloading. And what would the staff do half of the time? We have such a slick system, it works 90% of the time. The only time it fails is when masses of people walk in together and want loads of different food orders. Everyone's system wobbles then. I have come in to find the kitchen awash with dirty dishes and tables groaning under uncleared plates, but this is rare and quickly dealt with.

Some days the Tea Garden resembles a battle site. But very quickly the laborious process of getting everything upstairs, washed and put away happens. I'm always amazed how busy we can be and yet we are nearly always finished by 5pm – occasionally 5.30pm – and I could count on the fingers of one hand the times in twenty-eight years it has gone on after 6pm, even with a walkers' invasion at 4.30pm. But more of that later!

The youngsters have their job clearing the Tea Garden and rooms and then cleaning them. Supervisory staff cleans the kitchen, counter and loo. It's amazing how it all comes together, and we pull as a team and get it done.

I do feel sorry about some of the disgusting tables they have to reassemble and clean. The amount of mess a family makes amazes me – does this happen at home? Food on chairs, floor, walls. Does no one ever put a menu back in a menu holder? And while on this subject, vaguely, why won't people move a menu, hat, book, map, etc. so we can put a plate down? This is one of Susan's pet hates, as is the fact that they will never pass a dish we can't get to or move over. We in the catering profession go out of our way to help when out dining. As I have always maintained, 'Joe Public' should have to do a stint serving in a café or restaurant. Boy, would it make a difference to their behaviour and attitude to serving staff! This has changed over the years, though. At one time we were treated as if we hadn't a brain between us. Now, with unemployment so high, so many highly qualified, intelligent people are lucky if they can get a waiting job – so maybe there is a better understanding and we are treated a bit more like intelligent human beings.

Tipping is a very emotive subject. We are always amazed how few people do tip and it's not because of bad service. I think it is the daytime thing – this is backed up by my staff. Many have worked in evening establishments and received excellent tips.

We do get days when tips are really good, but not many. Or is it the wholefood crowd? I'm always amazed by people that wait for 5p change. £29.90 and they wait for 10p! I have to say the hospice jar, strategically placed, does get a lot of these.

Youngsters who work in catering do tip. My staff always do when out, they tell me. When you think that 15% is the percentage 'down south', the pound my staff get is a pittance – but they appreciate it.

I'm saying this because I'm always feeling sorry for my youngsters who I think deserve more. 'Percy Pig', my retirement fund, now collects the supervisors' tips, and we fairly frequently go out for a meal on it, a treat Blod and Susan have always appreciated. So, people, do tip, as it's just nowhere near the scale folks seem to do for evening dining. It's not to do with actual good service or food, it's very much a personal thing and I think a decreasing habit.

This chapter could not be complete without one person who has supported me staunchly from the off. My great support and help after I split with Ali was 'small Gwen', a mother in a million. She was so reliable and supportive, constantly helping not only at lunchtimes, but accompanying me on cash and carry and supermarket shops, and even helping me pick fruit – all this at over seventy. I always thought that I would continue till I was seventy, but the call of travel and adventure beckons too much after twenty-eight years of toil.

When Gwen gained her hygiene certificate she was so proud. It was her first and only qualification, all her life. It's a pity they do not have qualifications for wonderful mothers.

Walkers and Ramblers

Yes, I think I can speak with authority on this subject. Having dealt with them for twenty-eight years in all states and being a partner in my partner's walking company, I have decades of experience and real live incidents.

We have decided that there are two distinct groups: walkers – easier and, sorry, pleasanter, and ramblers – difficult and demanding. Susan summed it up one trying Sunday afternoon while ten were wanting to be served all at once: "You are very demanding!" Part of it is the herd instinct and part of it is "I want to be served now because I know that there are another twenty of us on their way and it will take so much time to serve us all." You can't double up on teapots? Who has twenty one-person teapots?

All wanting to pay at once, instead of letting us actually serve everyone. Sitting down and causing chaos as no one knows who's been served or what they are having, then giving the same order to two girls. Forgetting what the cake order was when it appears. Screaming for hot water when we are doing our damnedest to serve first time teapots.

"We only want one cup of tea."

"Can we have a pot for one and two cups?"

"Daphne only wants half a cup."

"I want a toasted tea-cake – what? You don't have any?"

"Have you no proper scones?"

"Are these all the cakes you have?" – despite there being a choice of at least eight varieties of cake – "Have you any proper cakes?"

Some are very thoughtful and will ask about removing boots – after all, we do have carpeted floors. Others just clump in, mud caked all over boots and trousers. With no apologies, they walk all around the café then wrap their muddy boots around the chair legs. Their trip to the toilet deposits mud all along the corridor and on the toilet floor. Their smelly waterproofs really *do* smell. This does put the general public off entering. Sometimes – yes, the noise and frenzied atmosphere as they take over totally stops anyone wishing to enter, or if they do they exit very quickly.

A little known fact they will never appreciate is that a group of twenty walkers frequently spends less than four members of the general public eating 'proper food and drink'.

There appears to be a general assumption that at 4.30pm, when closing time is 5pm, we will still be doing a full food menu. There is incomprehension that while I and, if I'm lucky, two other staff members are trying to cope with twenty plus drinks orders, I can also do hot varied food. In my wide experience of eating out after 3pm in small establishments, kitchens close, clean and don't produce food. In my 'walking hat' capacity I know walkers really struggle to get a drink and cake after 3pm. I do wonder where all the walkers get food and cakes from after 4pm. I haven't encountered any of these establishments.

Goodness knows, we do try and do miracles at Acorn – but the magic wand is getting worn out. Imagine in the summer what it is like to deal with two rooms upstairs and a Tea Garden that seats twenty five people!

The youngsters – who have to do the running around when they are there – not surprisingly get annoyed when being asked for extras after an order is delivered. These same people seem to take delight in sending them up and down the stairs at least three times. And of course they never tip them.

I have had many lovely, friendly, happy walkers and walk leaders who plan a walk, and then warn me of their impending walk date and time so we are ready and prepared for them. My partner is wonderfully trained to pre-book and then warn us when they are half an hour away so we have all the tables reserved and laid up. Yes! We are the café that always gets the 4.30pm walkers.

I'm afraid that some ramblers have the attitude that we should all be eternally grateful for their huge groups, disruption, noise, chaos and mess. But if somewhere else had tea and was open and 5p cheaper, they would go there.

I have had lots of walkers agree about the 'walkers' mentality' and ask how we put up with them and the 'herd instinct'. It brings out the worst in them!

The 4.30pm onslaught screaming at us "We have the bus to catch at five" does nothing to improve our response. One of my girls was reduced to tears by a rambler's rudeness, and my own worst display involved totally losing my rag to a particularly rude and loud lady.

Loo queuing is another walkers' trait. Why don't they start early, staggering their visits, not waiting until they are due to leave, resulting in a queue all down the corridor and getting 'annoyed' that we only have one toilet? If I've got the time and energy, I tell them the situation on entering – regulars know.

All this is avoided by groups that book, so that even if we don't know numbers we are pre-warned. Cups on tables, teapots ready and tables reserved. It works like a dream. The frequent excuse is that they can't say who will come in. Yes, the pub beckons for many – but having notice and staff is the vital thing when faced with groups.

Regular staff know how to react and we all get our 'systems' going. But many go into headless chicken mode, which does not help the situation or my tolerance level.

Have you ever thought how much room twenty backpacks take up? So we try and get those put in our office. I marvel at how lucky we are with all the room. How do the many poky little tearooms cope? And there are lots of them in Derbyshire and Wales.

Walking poles – the number of people we have run after to return them when they should have been attached to their back packs. Ditto hats, gloves and sun glasses.

Well, I've had my rant about ramblers. I can assure you that my friends are totally amazed and disgusted when I recall the incidents that we have had to put up with. Just mention 'walkers' to ex and present staff and note their faces!

We know Sundays are ramblers' days. Fortunately, their other day is Wednesday and I am closed. So we are always in half preparation for groups, and equally on Saturday afternoons. The early morning ones are rare and do catch me out as I am by myself then. I still say we will serve twelve people drinks more quickly than anywhere else.

The other invasion we dread is coach parties. Yes, most people can't cope with them, hence they are banned from so many places. My stairs act as a filter, but when the garden is open it proves challenging for us. Last year one group of oldies was hugely impressed by our speed, skill and humour. When one member of a coach group has braved the stairs, the others tend to follow. Fortunately I have got good vision from my kitchen window and I see them approaching. Kettles on, coffee machine going, and hey presto – I have them served within fifteen minutes. They are usually on a time table when it's a morning drop. Most are impressed by the efficiency and I tell them "This is as good as it gets" when they enter – meaning there's only me. I have even been known to get the more active to take some of the cups and pots out. Some ex-caterers even volunteer when they see the situation – good team work and no charge. They are all given a 'loo warning'. There's only one loo – so start now!

Joyous Moments

There are lovely people who, on walking into my Tea Garden, say, "Isn't this beautiful? Tranquil and natural and full of bird song."

If ever I get to hear that it is someone's birthday we always put a candle on their cake. It's such a small touch but so appreciated. If the right crowd are in, fellow diners will do a round of Happy Birthday. One lovely elderly lady this year chose to have her birthday afternoon tea with us, choosing Bara Brith as her birthday cake. She complimented us by saying that it was the best she had ever had, stating, "That's what I call a home-made cake!"

Different people rave about different cakes; it's all to do with taste. The carrot cake comes out top – but apricot slices, date slices, coconut orange and lemon cake and scones are also very popular. Parkin seems to bring back memories of bonfire nights, and people appreciate my wholemeal scones, saying, "How do you do such lovely risen wholemeal scones?" My bread pudding was the best ever tasted and had a 'sticky bottom' according to one customer. Flapjack – Susan is its number one fan. Her partner gets fed up with hearing when they are out, "It's not as good as Chris's". One lady from afar was so impressed with my Christmas cake that she came back the next year to purchase one – good job I still had one.

You either love or hate my pizza. Most children just pick the topping off – the base is wholemeal. My staff certainly laps it up. My soups are legendary. Well, I've done a good few thousand in my time. Not for us 'vegetable'. These are just a few: Spring Nettle, Aduki Bean, Pumpkin and Pinto, Cabbage and Caraway, Green Pea and Leek, Sprout and Walnut, Chestnut and Chickpea, Minted Shropshire Pea and Bungo.

My crumble mix seems to be appreciated by many people. "What do you put in it? It is so crunchy and tasty, and must be full of goodness" are frequent comments.

A small number of discerning people appreciate my healthy breakfast. Now, though, porridge is becoming more mainstream. It's not quite so unique.

Of course all the gluten free and intolerant folks are over the moon that they have the choice of cakes and something else to eat other than jacket potatoes. Vegans nearly pass out with shock when they actually have a choice of dishes, and sing my praises for many a long time.

Many people do "appreciate our décor" – yes, it's old fashioned, I suppose – mismatched little bits and pieces. People really do love the toilet, and one person was even in "awe" of the handle – yes, it was my replacement – bought by a customer to be more in keeping with the building.

There are people that just appreciate 'proper good coffee'. I certainly do. Not overpriced fluffy tasteless liquid, the good old fashioned milky coffee that still brings cries of delight.

The lovely girls and boys who have worked for me over the years have formed real friendships with me. They keep in touch; let me know of marriages, babies and other memorable events. I will actually have time to visit some of them in the many far flung places they have made home.

On my sixtieth birthday, they organised a surprise tea party. What a surprise it was, and I really did not have a clue about it. Seven of them made a wonderful presentation of two vouchers, one for theatre tickets – they know how I love the theatre – and one for dinner out. They were much enjoyed. They also bought a lovely pendant and earring set. The wonders of texts and emails and an organisational genius, Ruth Seager. Some of it was learnt at Acorn, I hope.

The support of many regulars and friends for Acorn has made it all worthwhile over the many years. Some customers come just once a year, sometimes every five years, but over the lifetime of Acorn I have got to know and appreciate their support and kindness. It's incredible how many people I recognise as previous visitors – and they are amazed that I can remember conversations we had years ago. I may not remember names but I always recognise a face.

We have been part of a lot of people's holidays for years – their meal or meals at Acorn. I have seen whole families grow up and go on their own way. People love coming back. They specially look us up and are amazed and delighted that I'm still here. Sometimes it's even "We came here ten years ago." They have not been in the area since, but are back now and come specially to find us. A friend tells me that when I am away on holiday and it's all closed up, she encounters many disappointed people retreating down the path.

Five years ago, I started putting yellow stickers on the inside of the toilet door with little sayings on them. My positive statements and thoughts for the day in the toilet give folks a lot of pleasure. They really seem to appreciate them, and even give me ones to add on. Yes, I do change them every few months, although I do have some old favourites. I find these inspirational and I hope they have the same effect on customers. My poster – 'Time for Women' – causes many a chuckle as people emerge from down the corridor. Here it is:

Time for Women

This letter was started by a woman like yourself in the hopes of bringing light relief to other tired and discontented women.

Unlike most chain letters this one does not cost anything. Just send a copy of this letter to five of your friends who are equally tired and discontented. Then, bundle up your husband or boyfriend, send him to the woman whose name appears at the top of the list and add your name to the bottom of the list.

When your name comes to the top of the list you will receive 16,877 men, and one of them is bound to be a hell of a lot better than the one you already have.

Do not break the chain. Have faith. One woman broke the chain and got her own sod back. At the time of writing, a friend of mine had already received 184 men. They buried her yesterday, but it took three undertakers 36 hours to get the smile off her face, and two days to get her legs together so they could close the coffin.

You Must Have Faith

I really appreciate the compliments I get about my figure and my energy – and say "You are truly what you eat." In my case that is correct. I believe passionately in the benefits of a wholefood and healthy diet, and the energy levels and benefits that this brings.

When I used to do homemade jams and marmalade, people noticed the difference between those and the mass produced versions which are invariably over sweet. Sometimes they could not tell what fruit I had used – and how good they thought gooseberry jam was! My fruit crumbles get the same reaction – I use little or no sugar in these, letting the true fruit flavour come through. Sometimes we mislabel them but no one seems to notice, or they are too polite to comment.

My four legged friends bring a smile to our faces. They crash through the door, into our dog room and await their reward for bringing the owner in – a dog biscuit – and the tail wags of appreciation always give me a buzz. Of course the owners are chuffed that the dog is welcome and not banished always to the garden.

Plants have been propagated from our plants that adorn the windows in both eating rooms. There must be relations of my magnificent Christmas cacti and stunning geraniums all over the world.

Two mountain bikers when they are on holiday stop for "some of my lovely food". Cyclists regularly call on Sunday mornings for a cake and a cuppa before carrying on for many more tens of miles.

The fans of my sugar free date slices come from far and wide – their delight makes up for the many pulled faces and leftovers of the uninitiated.

I do get a lot of thanks for being open every Sunday and on bank holidays. Every day we stay open after 4pm, and even in the depths of winter when the weather is foul I fly the hospitality banner and customers are glad of at least one place being open. I admit that I do close on certain dates for my own holiday – oh, the joys of holidays in the period between November and February! I've done most of the warmer destinations at that time of year over the past twenty-eight years.

The Recession

Well, we have weathered at least two recessions prior to this one, and the frightful times of the Foot and Mouth epidemic really were a living nightmare. I found it very hard to motivate the staff as so few people were coming in. My regulars must have kept us going, and people were so 'cabin bound' they came out even to a closed up countryside. I hope this country never again has to live through the crazy policies that were enacted during that horrendous period.

During the other two recessions we cut our cloth according to the garment. I never have had particular 'boom' years. We increased turnover year on year, apart from the year of Foot and Mouth. Too high an increase was fine when I acquired a full-time manageress. But I knew I couldn't cope solo with huge increases.

This recession of four years' standing is something else. We are fine as I'm very much into semi-retirement and so have cut back on everything. I feel so sorry for anyone seriously operating or just opening.

What we really have noticed is how everyone now drinks tap water – a thing unheard of four years ago – apart from sports folks or health conscious coffee/water drinkers. This really does affect our bottom line profit – a fact customers who still want to see 'small, independent cafés' don't seem to work out. It's become so common now; we are shocked if we sell a drink, and we know that "We will order something after" is a no-goer. It's not just us, as restaurant magazines have been doing long running press issues about it. Some of 'the orders' that we have been getting have made us incredible – scones for lunch, and one between two at that!

12.45pm: One lunch, two people. They study the menu for at least five minutes. One cup of coffee, one glass of tap water and two buttered toasts – £4.00! How does one keep going on that? 1.05pm: Twelve people in for lunch. One orders nothing at all, one soup, two buttered scones, two jam and cream scones, cafetière for two, two sardines on toast, two teas. Less than £25 for twelve people!

Another couple had a bowl of soup to share. Another one sandwich, one soup and one tea – to share!

Cakes and scones seem to have replaced lunches. People are having coffee and cakes at lunch time. Our soup is a meal in itself and has always been no problem – very rarely do we do a cake or dessert to follow now. Yet we still do get freak days when people actually eat a main course, cake or pudding and a drink – even I wouldn't still be here if some didn't.

I have always smiled over the salad issue. Years ago I stopped including it as so much was thrown away. The prices reflect this – I'm amazed when people ask, "Is it extra?" Yes, and listed as such. Our garnish is the equivalent of a salad. When we do a real 'side salad' people are warned, and then, if of the right ilk, they are amazed at how fantastic it is. Personally I don't order side salads when out. A bit of iceberg lettuce, tomato, cucumber and red onion is not a salad to me. And the prices they charge!

People really are watching every penny, and because so many 'deals' are about, they expect blood. It does make it harder for us; we are not competing on a level playing field.

High ethically-graded food does cost more, so straight away our Fair Trade tea and coffee are, at base line, more expensive. As I have explained, with flour, sugar and margarine I pay for top ethical products. Unfortunately with the 'general public' a lot of these considerations don't matter, and if they haven't seen the wholefood sign, they don't even know.

The bread is from an artisan baker, meat from locally reared animals, and with milk we support the local milkman. All the things that in the 'recession game' far too many people don't want to know.

With the cutting down of consumption, you would expect to see slim, well-toned, full of life bodies. Unfortunately, this does not seem to have happened! Is everyone then gorging on fast food, high calorie cheap junk food and drink?

This could get me on to my pet subject of obesity and where it will all end. At least folks seem conscious of it now – just not, as yet, doing a lot about it. Silly crash diets, not the eating for life policy they need to adopt. How often do you see wholefoods on TV chef programmes, in cookery books and eating establishments? Yet only this week the UN Food Commission said that to try and counter the horrendous predicted increase in cancer, we must eat more wholefood substances and reduce sugar intake. Have I, after twenty-eight years, at last been vindicated? Something I find really, really strange is when some people realise it's 'healthy food' and they don't want any of that! I cannot even start to get my head around this – perhaps making people pay for health services and rewarding people who really do try and care about the state of their body and mind is what is needed.

So, recession or no recession, cutting back is good – but not on the wrong things – and increasing the right things you eat. Yes, water is good for you; it's just not good for my bank balance.

On that subject I started charging for cups of hot water years ago. It was caused by a woman putting her own teabag in a cup of hot water. Yes, it was one of the twenty-five odd ones we had! Now, it is so common to be asked for a cup of hot water no one would query it, and it's the old resources saga. Serving a cup of hot water costs me.

Are You Still Open?

This was to have been the title for this book. If you only knew the times I have been asked that. It's going to be the epitaph on my grave. But an even more amusing and apt title came along after writing and proof reading the draft. So "Rants and Recipes" it is.

We have bets that it will be the first question asked by everyone coming up the stairs after 4pm. I have even been asked it at 10am, 11am, lunchtime and twenty to three. Is there something I have missed about other cafés' opening times? If the gates are open, the sign shows 'open', lights are on and staff are about, I reckon so! I know a lot of establishments are negligent, leave signs out, doors open etc. – but not us. It is incredible, even with the door pulled to, lights off and café in darkness, I have still had folks creep up the stairs – nearly scaring us both to death.

I can understand the 4pm rush; when we are out, I'm getting frantic to get a tea and cake at 3.30pm, as an awful lot of cafés do shut at afternoon tea time. We do half of our business regularly after 4pm. I always say people find us then. Walkers never come in before 4pm – and that's it, I just cracked it. It's why cafés do shut. They can't cope with the mass onslaught and dirty boot syndrome. Many, many people are very grateful that we do stay open until 5pm. The other strange thing is that, on being told that we close at 5pm, some people take ages to decide on a mere drink and cake, and then they sit and sit and sit! One couple started getting newspapers out at 4.50pm. At 5.30pm I explained I closed at 5pm.

When the vacuum cleaner is going, the cashing up has been done and there is still no movement we have to ask them to leave. After nine hours, I do think I am entitled to a life. I have a theory: they buy a tea and a cake and they think that they have hired the place indefinitely. The people that I have let in at nearly 5pm and served would fill a book. I'm still waiting for this obliging service when we are out. We have had doors and signs slammed in our faces many, many times at 4pm. I have been known to leave people in the Tea Garden and ask them to shut the gate onto the street when they leave, please – at 5.30pm. Sometimes even we aren't open long enough – as I'm taking signs in even I have my limit. One night I received a load of abuse at 5.15pm on a bank holiday Monday from two late arrivals. In my tired state they were lucky not to receive any abuse back! I never cease to be amazed how people just stroll in at 4.45pm and order, even trying for hot food some days. What world do these people live in? The number of people that are amazed that we are open on Sundays! It has always been one of our busiest days. I don't understand any tourist café that doesn't open on bank holidays – even though I hate them.

Bank holidays are not what they used to be, and I'm very glad. I still recall one truly horrendous Easter Monday, the Tea Garden awash with dirties, people queuing to get in and upstairs completely full and gridlocked. I think people do completely different things on bank holidays now. We know it will be horrendous anywhere 'public'. I know that we, as a family, never went out then, for that particular reason – and that was fifty years ago.

It's an amazing situation – at 3.50pm we can be empty, at 4.15pm full. I used to joke with one of the girls every Saturday for about two years about this, and I had to get her on the bus for 5.10pm. We certainly learnt to fly around the café and work smart and fast. I have threatened to have a sign on my forehead after 4pm "Yes we are STILL open". We think people follow each other down the street and it goes out on the bush telegraph. It really does have to be seen and heard to be believed. A lone couple can be enjoying a quiet cuppa, and whoosh! They are engulfed by fellow diners. It's even worse for them if it's a group of walkers. This is when we really have to keep on top of the washing up, and have cleaned our kitchen and be fully prepared for close down – otherwise, we could still be at it at it at 6pm.

"Are you open?" extends to closed days and holidays. When I lived in the flat above the café, frequently on my closed day I would wait behind closed doors as I heard people standing outside on the path saying "Oh no, she's closed!", the sign on the door relaying this information, despite the fact that I had closed on a Wednesday for twenty-eight years. I used to dread venturing out onto the path and being ambushed. I have been asked would I open up as they have come all the way from Bath!

Customers

Dirtiest floor ever – 31 March 2013. It must have been the weather and walkers. The poor staff did a splendid job but it was hard work.

You would not credit the amount of mud, sheep poo, stones and food that can be deposited on a floor. This is on top of our immediate use of the dust pan and brush under particularly bad tables. We have been known to vacuum twice, even three times some afternoons before it is finally clean and ready for the next day. I have always, always insisted on getting everything finished that night. We never know what the next day will throw at us. There is a strange phenomenon: the one morning I have no staff, it will go crazy. Or I let staff go early and it erupts. When I have staff the café is quiet, and when I am by myself, it is busy. I joke if it's been busy, because as soon as my staff come in, it will go quiet.

I can always spot the 'jam and cream scones' and milky coffee mugs and hot chocolate customers. They are usually at least three stones overweight, nearly expire as they climb the stairs and joke about their enforced disability. I see the results of the diabetes explosion every day. They seem clueless about diet, apart from 'no sugar'. Very few seem to have cottoned on to the wholefood help side and don't want to help themselves. It's easier to be labelled, pop a pill and then they don't have to take responsibility for their own body.

It goes the other way with thin, pallid, lifeless individuals who can't eat a cake and feel they have to justify their denial.

Over the years I have seen the strong ties between food, emotions, control, self-worth and self-hate. In some cases it's bewildering and frightening; controlling mothers, daughters, husbands, wives, girlfriends, boyfriends. Freud would have had a field day here.

When we are busy serving and preparing food, people always stand up and want to pay. Nothing will have been happening three minutes before, and nor will it after. Customers cannot work out that when we have four tables, we need to get one order into the kitchen to start the process. If everybody takes ages and it all comes in together, everyone waits that much longer. For the last table it seems like a lifetime, and those are always the ones that only have half an hour's parking left.

The new trend, the last ten years, is for people to be on mobile phones: answering them at top volume and staying in the room; playing with texts, games or heaven knows what when they are actually with someone. Amazing! I'm loath to put another notice up – 'Where did manners go?' I have been known to take my phone to the table to communicate the presentation of their food; it usually raises a smile, perhaps makes them think. I also find it amazing when I hear people talking in the toilet when they have gone in on their own, and I realise they are talking on their mobile phone! It's not an S.O.S! As for "Are you on Wi-Fi?" my friends fall about laughing when they hear this. If you knew my lack of technical skill! You can go elsewhere and occupy a table for one coffee for at least one and a half hours!

Yes, we are frequently used as an office. Folks on their laptops, holding informal meetings of two to four people, with one pot of tea, for two hours. It's a good thing that I have lots of space and we are not a 'bums on seats' establishment.

Our favourite is the toilet trick. Four people all go separately, over seven minutes, to the toilet, and no one has given anyone else in their group their order. So everyone waits and that order gets knocked down the growing stack. We laugh about this when we are out, and I always leave my order before I go to the toilet. Blod's pet hate is the man always disappearing to the loo as the food is served. Our problem is often that we serve the food too quickly and people are still doing the toilet drama.

"Such fun, keep breathing!" This is my pet phrase when staff go into panic mode and then forget to breathe. It's kept most people reasonably upright over the years. I have to thank a wonderful customer over many years – now sadly not with us – for this phrase. He had sussed the scene at Acorn.

I have to say a big "thank you" to all the wonderful, lovely customers over the years who have passed through Acorn's doors, some becoming friends, others sharing stories, joy and pains, appreciating my food and my 'baby', as one friend called Acorn. It's made it all worthwhile, forming my stories, laughs, friendships; it's given me the chance to work with two super supportive friends. Amazingly, we are still friends after all the stress and work that Acorn produces.

It is amazing when I meet new people or I'm in different places and I get to talk about my profession, and Acorn comes up. It's not that I only socialise with 'wholefood friends'. I have even been in restaurants in London and Madeira and met a person who has been into Acorn.

I met my dear partner of eight years' standing due to Acorn and walkers! So walkers do bring unexpected pleasure and amazing opportunities. From this particular partnership has come some very good business for Acorn and Secrethills.

Sometimes I think Acorn is a social club as I spend so much time talking with one friend and another. Blod said that friends still keep coming in even on the days that I have off. Others arrive from a great distance and still miss me. Some friends do seem incapable of seeing we are very busy and they keep talking as they wander around following me. Others have been roped into washing up, serving and clearing tables – for which I am always very grateful.

Peggy and Family

A special mention must be included to a very special lady, Peggy Puplett, and her family. She is sadly now departed from this world, but was a lovely, lovely customer over many years.

We initially bonded over dogs. Peggy and I used to meet quite often around 7am while walking our respective dogs. Then Peggy became a Saturday regular, coming in for soup, fresh fruit salad and Earl Grey tea. A very healthy mixture! No wonder she lived a healthy life into her nineties. She never baulked at the many and varied soups, and loved my Spring Nettle. She was always keen to try a new one and she certainly sampled many.

For many years she came in on Christmas Eve with her son and lovely family. It was a late, late lunch – 4pm, always giving me the 'last trader closing on Christmas Eve' title. It became a family and Acorn tradition. They used to say their Christmas began at this time. The pre-ordered quiche went with them for Boxing Day. They all so thoroughly enjoyed the meal and mulled wine – it was a real pleasure, now sadly missed.

When it became impossible for Peggy to climb the stairs, it was a very sad event. I used to pop around with some soup and a cake on a Sunday afternoon when I had cover. She was always so pleased to see me and still interested in Acorn.

Betty

Known to everyone at Acorn, she has been my most loyal, frequent customer since she discovered me back in April 1999 on moving to Shrewsbury. Delighted that we accepted dogs in Acorn, she would bring her dog, Kinny, and they became two of our happiest customers. Kinny dragged Betty in off the street; she hit our door at high speed and the tinkling bell always announced their entry.

Once a huge bull terrier followed them in. This beast was trying to mount little Kinny. Betty was trying to get in to us and remove this large dog. Crash, bang, went our door, Betty shouting "Help!" and me shouting and racing to the door, fearing an armed raid. Finding Betty with Kinny pinned to the door, I dragged the bull terrier off and into my garden and shut him in there. He was collarless but fortunately good natured, and I left him to go and contact the police. I gave them all the details then I administered Arnica to Betty and gave a biscuit to Kinny, who was undeterred by the whole event, unlike Betty and I who were quite shaken by it. When I returned to the garden I saw that the said bull terrier had chewed his way through my gate and escaped. None of us saw him again or heard any more about him. But my gate was the proof that it really had all happened – in a frantic five minutes!

Apple Fayre

For twenty years we catered for the local Apple Fayre, held every two years in October, the inspiration of the Green Party councillor John Lloyd, who organised it over all those years. Back in 1993, we took over the catering side of it. Had it not been for my wonderful, loyal volunteers and friends and sister, when she was alive, it would not have been possible to man. It just grew and grew over the years, in range and quantity of dishes. At the final one in 2012 I peaked at over forty apple dishes. It is amazing what you can do with apples; such a versatile fruit – sweet, savoury, cakes and soup.

This event resulted in the publication by a local artist and book binder, Peter Andrew Jones, of my book 'Apple Fayre'. He produced, with my recipes, a beautifully hand-made limited edition book. Only two hundred copies were produced, with recipes and paintings all dedicated to apples. It was a fitting tribute to our Apple Fayre.

Over the years I increased the number of dishes and amazed the customers. It became quite a focal point to attend, to try these amazing dishes – new ones, old favourites and surprises. A wonderful display of British apples, always beautifully presented, welcomed visitors as they entered. It really was a splendid sight when it was all set out.

The day always kept us frantically busy, from the 5.30am start for me with fresh apple and cheese scones. Need I say the months of previous preparation of cakes and frozen desserts was eventually worth it all? The tremendous amount of extra work it generated just melted away.

In 2012, I told John it was going to be my final one. We had been one of the first places to celebrate and promote the wonderful variety of English apples and to run an Apple Fayre. Since then, they have become common in many towns in autumn, but I have seen nothing to compare with the variety and amount we produced. So we went out on a high after the 2012 Apple Fayre.

•

Recipes

Introduction

I had to be quite clinical about which recipes to include. I have so many. So I arrived at ones really relevant to Acorn: some given by special friends, others I've devised, and favourites.

There's a mix of ten favourite cakes, ten of the more unusual soups that I devised and serve in the café, ten of the more different vegetarian dishes – but not too exotic – and then ten of the special dishes that I serve at Acorn, from my hot spiced apple mixture to my wholemeal pastry.

I have presumed when writing that people know how to cook. I've assumed a knowledge of whisking, folding, baking trays, etc. My ingredient measures are pounds and ounces – I was brought up with them. The cup measurements are from my New Zealand travels. A few grams may have crept in!

I always use a pressure cooker for cooking dried beans and peas because of the large quantities that I process, but because of the small quantities that the people reading my recipes will require and the ready availability of tinned beans and peas, I recommend using tinned ones.

I have found nothing can be timed perfectly. Ovens vary so much and also people's tastes, so I disclaim any results! Mine worked for twenty-eight years – so they are certainly well tried and tested!

I wish everyone good luck – they all served me well for many years and I would like them to be officially recorded. What a terrible waste if they weren't – where else can you get wholemeal scones like the ones at Acorn?

Happy Acorn Café wholemeal cooking.

Soups

Here are a few of my classic but unusual soups. Some summer ones, lots of winter ones – the best time for soup. I have literally made thousands of soups over the years and I maintain there's not much you can't put in soup. Unfortunately, I do tend to use what we have, seasonal or what I fancy. So it's been quite hard to record specific measurements and ingredients.

I always start off by sautéing onion and usually garlic in oil. The oil is always sunflower. I never use stock cubes – I rely on the ingredients, herbs and spices. Salt and pepper addition by customers has driven me mad. They never taste the soup but proceed to add lots of black pepper and streams of salt. I have been known to say, "Excuse me, I've spent ages lovingly making that". One day, I thought one woman was never going to stop grinding pepper – the soup was tasty, but all she would have tasted was pepper.

Most of the soups we puree now as most people prefer 'mushed' soups. Blod was horrified when one day she left sliced mushrooms in the mushroom soup and then discovered the customer had left all the mushrooms on the side! I did tell her they would be left – folks like their vegetables smashed to 'no trace'. My soups are spicy but not chilli hot. I have explained this elsewhere. Many folks, like myself, do not like chilli. So many dishes now have chilli as a basic ingredient. I think it ruins all the flavour – it's just hot!

All the recipes contained in this section make a generous portion for 4 people.

Spiced Lentil Soup

1 large onion
1 large carrot
1 large parsnip
½ tsp ground cumin
½ tsp ground coriander
½ tsp turmeric
1 400g tin chopped tomatoes
6 oz red lentils
3 tbs sunflower oil
1 clove garlic
1 ½ pints water (approximately)
Salt and pepper

Method
1   Heat oil and add chopped onion and crushed garlic.
2   Sauté until translucent, add spices and fry for 1–2 minutes.
3   Add chopped carrots and parsnip. Stir/sauté for 5 minutes.
4   Add lentils, salt, pepper and boiled water.
5   Bring to the boil, simmer until lentils are cooked. Cool and puree.

This is a lovely, comforting winter warming soup – vegan, dairy free and full of wholesome ingredients.

Aduki Bean Soup

4 oz dried Aduki beans or 400g can
1 large onion
1 stick celery
1 large carrot
1 clove garlic
2 tbs oil
1 400g tin chopped tomatoes
2 tbs tomato puree
1 bay leaf
½ tsp thyme
Salt and pepper
1½ pts boiled water
Chopped parsley to garnish

Method

1   If using dried beans, soak overnight and cook the next morning. Keep liquid.
2   Heat oil and sauté the crushed garlic and chopped onion for 5 minutes. Add celery and carrots and stir.
3   Add tomatoes, puree, herbs, water and cooked beans.
4   Add extra water as required. Simmer for ¾ hour.
5   Served topped with lots of chopped parsley.

The Chinese call aduki beans 'red wonder' beans as they are so full of goodness. The liquid you produce when cooking is supposed to be good for the kidneys.

Chestnut and Chickpea Soup

1 large can chestnut puree
2 sticks celery
½ lb chickpeas or 400g can
2 medium onions
1 clove garlic
Bay leaf, pinch of nutmeg, salt and pepper
1 ½ pts boiled water
Few sprigs of parsley

Method
1   If using dried chickpeas, soak overnight and then cook.
2   Heat oil and sauté the crushed garlic and chopped onion. Add celery and stir.
3   Add chestnut puree – melted down with boiled water.
4   Add cooked chickpeas and seasoning.
5   Simmer for 20 minutes. Cool and puree. Leave a few whole chickpeas to garnish.
6   Sprinkle chopped parsley over each bowl of soup.

This is one of our seasonal Christmas specials. We seem to have been using chestnut puree before most folk. I have to think now to buy it well in advance of 25 December.

Pumpkin and Pinto Soup

2 lbs inside of pumpkin – chopped (discard the seeds and fibres,
   retain the shell for lantern)
1 large onion
1 large potato
2 sticks celery
1 400g tin chopped tomatoes
1 400g tin Pinto beans or ½ lb dried – soaked and cooked
1 ½ pints water
½ tsp caraway seeds
Salt and pepper
2 tbs sunflower oil

Method

1   Sauté chopped onion in hot oil, add chopped celery
    and chopped potato. Stir and cook for 5 minutes.
2   Add pumpkin, tomatoes, caraway seeds, seasoning
    and water.
3   Simmer together for 20 minutes, puree, then add
    beans and simmer for 10 minutes. Adjust seasoning,
    serve hot.

*A good soup to serve for your Halloween party – uses up the
insides of the pumpkin and warms you all up.*

Shropshire Minted Pea Soup

1 medium packet frozen peas or 4 lbs fresh peas in pods
1 large onion
2 large potatoes
Bunch of fresh mint to taste
Salt and pepper
1 ½ pints water
Oil to sauté

Method
1   Sauté chopped onion and potatoes for 10 minutes.
2   Add chopped mint, peas, seasoning and water.
3   Simmer for 20 minutes, then puree.
4   Serve with a swirl of yoghurt and a mint leaf – if not
     vegan or dairy allergic.

*A lovely refreshing summer soup, always a favourite. I'm afraid
I do cheat now and use frozen peas. Too many years of shelling!
Frozen peas really are harvested at their best – you get no 'old ones'.*

Spring Nettle Soup

1 large onion
2 large potatoes
2 sticks celery
½ carrier bag of young spring nettles (picked with rubber gloves from a 'safe' area)
Salt and pepper
Pinch of nutmeg
1 ½ pints water*

Method

1   Thoroughly wash and sort nettles – you only want tops, no woody stalks.
2   Chop onion and sauté in oil. Add chopped celery and potatoes, sauté for a further 10 minutes.
3   Add nettles and seasoning and 1 ½ pts boiled water.
4   Bring to the boil and simmer for 20 minutes.
5   Puree finely and adjust seasoning.
6   You can add a swirl of cream before serving.

* This can be substituted with ½ milk and ½ water for a creamier consistency.

Wonderful use of nettles – from spray free and animal free zones. Full of iron, vitamin C and minerals – and it looks so healthy.

Lentil, Tomato and Carrot Soup

1 large onion
2 sticks celery
4 large carrots
1 clove garlic
1 400g can chopped tomatoes
2 tbs tomato puree
4 oz red lentils (dried)
½ tsp paprika
Salt and pepper
1 ½ pints water
Oil to sauté

Method

1   Sauté chopped onion, celery and crushed garlic for 10 minutes.
2   Add grated carrot and sauté for a further 5 minutes.
3   Add tinned tomatoes, tomato puree, seasoning and then lentils – stir.
4   Add boiled water – as needed, depends if you like thick or thin soup!
5   Cook until lentils are very soft. Puree.

Beetroot and Potato Soup

2 large onions
2 sticks celery
½ tsp paprika
Salt and pepper
1 ½ pints water
1 clove garlic
1 lb potatoes
1 lb cooked beetroot or a bunch of fresh beetroot, cooked

Method

1   Sauté chopped onions and garlic for 5 minutes.
2   Add chopped celery, potatoes and seasoning.
3   Chop or grate beetroot (messy!) and add to pan with boiled water.
4   Simmer for 20 minutes. Adjust seasoning.
5   Puree to serve, with a swirl of yoghurt if wanted.

A very impressive coloured soup, full of anti-oxidants and fibre and very tasty. It's amazing how many people have not tasted beetroot soup – either up for a try, or "No, I don't like!" thinking of the pickled version, which is a totally different taste.

Spiced Yellow Pea Soup

8 oz split yellow peas (soaked overnight)
2 large onions
2 sticks celery
1 clove garlic
½ tsp ground cumin
½ tsp ground coriander
½ tsp garam masala
Black pepper and salt
1 ½ pints boiled water
Oil to sauté

Method
1   Cook peas and retain liquid.
2   Sauté chopped onions, celery and crushed garlic.
    Add spices, sauté to seal for 5 minutes.
3   Add pea liquid and boiled water.
4   Simmer for 20 minutes. Check seasoning.
5   Cool and puree.

You add the spices to your taste. This is crying out to be served with granary garlic bread!

Cream of Lettuce Soup

1 bunch spring onions
2 lbs potatoes
2 sticks celery
1 ½ lbs lettuce (whatever is in the garden – Iceberg, Little Gem
   or Crispy)
1 tsp chives, fresh, to garnish
Salt and pepper
½ pint milk
1 pint water

Method
1 Prepare and chop onions – sauté.
2 Add chopped potatoes and celery – sauté.
3 Wash and shred lettuce, add to the pan.
4 Add milk and water – stir.
5 Simmer for 20 minutes. Adjust seasoning.
6 Puree to serve.
7 Could add a swirl of cream and a few chopped fresh chives.

Good way to use up surplus lettuce if you are a gardener!
A lovely, light, fresh summer soup.

Vegetarian Dishes

The choice of which recipes to include in this section was, again, very difficult. I must have made hundreds of various dishes over the years. Many were experiments and trials. When presented with seasonal vegetables and surplus produce, I produced a new dish!

I have included some with ingredients such as tofu that some people seem afraid to use, or do not know what to do with. Well, here are some ideas.

There are not too many 'cheesy ones' as that is the vegetarian opt out. They feature the use of nuts that are so versatile and under used in vegetarian cooking. My nut roast is no longer the Christmas joke and is very popular.

I have a particular love of beans and lentils, but know a lot of people who don't, or have digestive problems with them. I challenge any 'normal' person not to enjoy the Beanie Cheese Crunch or Lentil and Mushroom Gratin if presented as a meal!

Mock Goose was always one of the Christmas spectaculars, and this huge en croute object could be a goose breast – with a little imagination!

Go for it! Happy experimenting and tasting! The recipes here should make four generous portions.

Winter Chestnut Hotpot

4 oz dried chestnuts, soaked overnight, or 1 400g tin
½ lb shallots
½ lb sprouts – small
½ lb carrots
2 sticks celery
¼ lb button mushrooms
1 clove garlic
¼ tsp mustard powder
1 tbs Tamari sauce
2 tbs chopped parsley

Method
1   If using dried chestnuts, boil or pressure cook.
2   Prepare all vegetables and chop, but leave sprouts whole.
3   Heat oil and sauté onion and garlic, then add celery and carrots.
4   Add mustard powder, Tamari sauce and cooked chestnuts with ½ pt of their cooking liquid.
5   Simmer for 20 minutes. Add prepared mushrooms and whole sprouts. Cook adjusting liquid levels. Sprouts should still have 'crunch'.
6   Serve on a bed of brown rice.

One of my Christmas specials. I always think chestnuts are Christmassy! Good use of sprouts – even 'non-sprout' eaters have enjoyed this!

Beanie Cheese Crunch

3 oz each of dried butterbeans, black-eye, red kidney – or whatever mix you like – or 1 400g can of mixed beans
1 large onion
3 sticks celery
1 clove garlic
1 400g tin chopped tomatoes
1 tbs tomato puree
½ tsp paprika
2 carrots

Topping
3 oz wholemeal breadcrumbs
2 oz grated Cheddar cheese (extra mature)
1 oz sesame seeds
1 oz sunflower seeds

Method
1   If using dried beans, soak overnight and then cook on day of use.
2   Chop onion, celery, carrots and garlic. Sauté in oil until soft.
3   Add tomatoes, tomato puree, spices, then beans. Stir.
4   Simmer for 20 minutes.
5   Transfer to baking dish (shallow casserole dish).
6   Mix all topping ingredients together and sprinkle over the top of the beans, then bake at 190°C for 20 minutes until golden and crunchy.

A lovely, nourishing and hearty winter's supper dish. Serve with green salad. Topping can be adapted for gluten- and wheat-free diets.

Lentil and Mushroom Gratin

1 onion
1 carrot
2 sticks celery
1 clove garlic
8 oz red lentils
2 tbs oil
2 tbs soya sauce
1 pt water
Salt and pepper
4 oz grated cheese – omit if vegan

Mushroom filling
1 oz sunflower margarine
1 clove garlic
½ lb mushrooms
3 tbs chopped parsley

Method

1   Heat oil in pan, sauté prepared chopped onions, carrots, celery and garlic. Stir until soft.

2   Add other ingredients and simmer in water – lentils should be cooked but not too soggy and wet. Stir in half of the cheese.

3   For the topping – melt margarine, add crushed garlic, chopped mushrooms, seasoning and parsley. Sauté for 5 minutes.

4   Place half of the lentil mixture in a flat oven proof dish, top with a middle layer of the mushroom mix, then top that with the lentil mix.

5   Sprinkle the remaining cheese on top.

6   Bake at 190°C for 20–30 minutes, until golden.

7   Serve with a green salad and granary garlic bread.

The cheese topping can be omitted and sesame or sunflower seeds used instead for dairy-free or vegan diets.

Parsnip and Potato Bake

2 medium onions
3 medium parsnips
4 medium potatoes
1 pint milk
1 clove garlic
2 tbs maize meal/cornflour
Salt and cayenne pepper
¼ lb grated cheese
½ pint water
Sliced tomatoes for garnish

Method

1   Peel and thinly slice all vegetables.
2   Heat oil, crush the garlic and sauté in the oil with the sliced vegetables. Stir and gradually add the water. Simmer for 15 minutes.
3   Whilst cooking, make a cheese sauce.
4   Drain vegetables when cooked. Mix with half of the cheese sauce.
5   Put into greased ovenproof dish and top with the remaining cheese sauce. Sprinkle with grated cheese.
6   Bake at 190°C for 20–30 minutes. Put sliced tomatoes on top for the last 10 minutes.

Nut Roast

12 tinned tomatoes
1 lb chopped Brazil nuts
9 oz wholemeal breadcrumbs
4 tbs soya flour
4 tbs rolled oats
9 tbs quinoa flour or chestnut flour
4 tsp basil
2 tsp thyme

Method

1   Mash tomatoes, add all the above ingredients and mix
    well.
2   Spoon into a greased, lined loaf tin – however many or
    whatever size you want.
3   Bake at 180°C for 20–35 minutes until cooked.
4   Cool and turn out.

Delicious sliced and warmed with a mixed salad.

*I've been doing this recipe since I opened and it's always been
enjoyed – even the people that have never had nut roast before.
I have had to vary the flour – quinoa or chestnut – depending
on what I've been able to obtain. Supplies have improved
considerably recently.*

Mock Goose or Chestnut Wellington

Batch of wholemeal pastry
(see *Special Acorn Dishes*)
1 large onion
2 sticks celery
1 head fennel
1 oz flame raisins
2 oz wholemeal breadcrumbs
1 large tin of chestnut puree

2 oz whole cooked chestnuts
Pinch of thyme, sage, cinnamon
1 clove garlic
Oil to sauté
1 egg – for glazing

Method

1   Chop onion and celery. Crush the garlic and sauté all in the hot oil.
2   Add chopped fennel and spices. Melt down the chestnut puree and stir.
3   When melted, switch off heat and stir in all the other ingredients. Then leave to cool.
4   Roll out the pastry to put filling in the centre and cut one inch strips down the two sides.
5   Plait one side, then the other on top of the filling to encase it all, sealing each with beaten egg and then glazing the whole item. If this is for vegans, use thinned tahini paste to seal.
6   Bake at 180°C for 30–40 minutes. until golden.
7   Serve with salad and jacket potatoes if people have a hearty appetite.

This is one of my Christmas specials – hence the 'Mock Goose' title. It looks very impressive and a bit different and spectacular for vegetarians at Christmas.

Chickpea, Butterbean and Tahini Casserole

2 medium onions
2 cloves garlic
1 450g tin chickpeas
1 450g tin butterbeans
1 tbs Tahini
1 tsp basil
¼ tsp nutmeg
1 lb fresh or 1 tin chopped tomatoes
Oil for sautéing

Method

1   Sauté the onion and garlic in hot oil.
2   Combine everything else making sure the Tahini is well mixed.
3   Put in the casserole dish and add more liquid if required. Put in the oven and cook for 30 minutes or on top of the stove simmer for 20 minutes.
4   Serve on a bed of brown rice and with a green salad and olives.

Tofu and Vegetable Biryani

2 large carrots
2 sticks celery
2 medium onions
1 head of broccoli
1 red pepper
1 packet tofu
2 oz cashew nuts
1 ½ pints water
2 cloves garlic
Small piece of root ginger
1 tsp turmeric
1 tsp curry powder
½ tsp cinnamon
2 tbs chopped coriander
1 400g tin chopped tomatoes
8 oz long grain brown rice

Method

1   Drain tofu and cut into bite-sized pieces. Toss in spices and leave overnight.
2   Chop onion, carrot, celery. Crush garlic and sauté all in hot oil.
3   Add peppers, stir in spice tofu and chopped ginger. Fry for 2 minutes.
4   Stir in rice and add water, broccoli.
5   Simmer gently for 30 minutes or put in the oven at 180°C for 40 minutes.
6   Meanwhile toast cashews and when serving scatter on top with the coriander and serve with mango chutney.

Italian-Style Tofu

1 large onion
1 large red pepper
1 stick of celery
1 packet of tofu – chopped
1 400g tin chopped tomatoes
1 tbs tomato puree
3 tbs red wine
Pinch of paprika
1 crushed clove of garlic
½ tsp dried basil

Method

1   Marinate the tofu overnight in the tomato puree, red wine, paprika, garlic and basil.
2   Sauté the onion, celery and pepper.
3   Add the marinated tofu and juices – stir.
4   Add tinned tomatoes and puree and ¼ pt of water and gently simmer for 15 minutes. Adjust seasoning.
5   Serve on a bed of wholemeal spaghetti or other pasta, sprinkled with Parmesan if desired.

I thought I should include some tofu dishes which are good for menopausal women! Sadly it is rarely used or seen on menus apart from speciality restaurants and cafes.

I was complimented by a Japanese lady on this particular recipe – so 'it don't get much better than that!'

Chilli Bean Hotpot

1 400g can red kidney beans or dried, soaked beans
2 medium onions
2 medium carrots
1 stick of celery
1 small swede
1 400g can chopped tomatoes
2 tbs tomato puree
3 tbs red wine
2 oz quinoa
½ tsp basil
½ tsp coriander
Chilli powder – to your taste!
½ lemon

Method

1   Heat oil in pan and add crushed garlic, chopped onion and celery. Sauté for 6 minutes.
2   Add spices and herbs, then add remaining chopped vegetables. Cook for 6 minutes to seal the flavours.
3   Add the tomatoes, tomato puree, beans, red wine and stir thoroughly. Bring to the boil and simmer for 30 minutes.
4   Wash quinoa and steam for 10 minutes. Then add to the chilli mix, adjusting the seasoning and liquid levels.
5   Squeeze half a lemon into the mix before you serve. Can be served on a bed of brown rice but it is fairly complete as it is.

This is a super nutritious meal with the high protein content of quinoa.

Special Acorn Dishes

This chapter contains my very special Acorn dishes, absolutely unique to me as I created most of them and adapted others. I'm very proud that they have withstood the test of time. The hot spiced apple drink people remember from previous visits.

My Christmas cake is still thought of as one of the finest recipes and I have passed it on to many people.

The scones and pastry are not easy to perfect! But practise and persist! It goes without saying that they are second nature to me as I have been turning them out for years.

The crumble mix was perfected out of trying to cater for wheat-free diets. Also to make a more nutritious non-sweet topping for seasonal fruit.

My Seville marmalade comes from wanting to provide 'real marmalade', not over-sweet and with a real tang.

The mulled wine sprung from a hospitality gesture at Christmas well before mulled wine became trendy again. The aroma adds a seasonal touch as it floats through the restaurant and down the stairs and into the street.

Christmas Cake – Acorn Style

6 tbs brandy or rum
1 ½ lbs currants, sultanas and raisins
¼ lb chopped dates
¼ lb cherries – natural
3 oz chopped walnuts
6 oz wholemeal flour
2 tsp baking powder
1 tsp mixed spice
½ tsp each of ginger, nutmeg and cinnamon powder
8 oz butter
8 oz dark muscovado sugar
Grated rind of orange or lemon
4 eggs
2 tbs marmalade
1 tbs dark treacle

Method

One week before making the cake, soak the fruit in the alcohol and put in an airtight container. Shake daily.

1 Cream the softened butter with the sugar, spices and fruit peel.
2 Mix in fruit, eggs and nuts. Fold in the flour and all the remaining dry ingredients.
3 Line a round or square 8" fruit cake tin. Put brown paper around the outside of the tin. Secure this with string – this prevents over browning of the sides.
4 Spoon in the mixture, make a dip in the centre.
5 Sprinkle a mixture of nuts, glace fruits and sesame seeds on top of the cake.

6   Bake at 130°C for 2 hours, then 110°C for 1 hour
    until a skewer inserted in the centre comes out clean.
    Switch off the oven and leave the cake in the oven.
7   Next day remove the cake from the oven and take out
    of the tin.

Store in foil until required.

*I have made this cake every year for thirty plus years. It makes
a gloriously rich, moist festive cake. A dear friend gave me the
recipe over fifty five years ago – it still ages nicely.*

*I used to give small versions of it to 'special customers' at
Christmas time and they all loved it.*

Hot Spiced Apple Drink

¾ tsp ground cinnamon
¼ tsp ground nutmeg
¼ tsp allspice
Apple juice

Method

1   Shake together all the spices and store in a small (hotel type) individual jam or marmalade pot.
2   Put a pinch of this mixture in the bottom of a china mug and add apple juice.
3   Heat in a microwave or saucepan on the stove to your required temperature for drinking. Stir.

This is a real winter warmer, so easy but a real 'different' drink for the long cold winter months.

We have done this drink for twenty eight years – since I invented it on our opening menu and it's still as popular as ever.

Garlic Bread

1 clove garlic (large) or 2 depending on your taste
250g sunflower margarine(I use dairy-free non-hydrogenated)
½ stick granary bread

Method
1   Crush garlic clove/s
2   Mix garlic thoroughly in margarine.
3   Spread generously over two sides of sliced granary stick (length-wise.)
4   Ideally bake in oven, or put in the microwave to just melt the fat – if over done in a microwave, it will go hard. Serve immediately.

We have served this with soup, if required, since our opening day. Very popular with many people. I have never understood why more cafes don't offer this option!

Belgian Cake

1 lb bran flakes
½ lb crushed Rich Tea biscuits
6 oz chopped walnuts
¾ lb syrup
3 oz raisins
4 oz cherries – natural
12 oz margarine
12 tbs drinking chocolate (good quality)

Method

1   Crush biscuits and bran flakes
2   Grease a 12" square baking tray. I line it with greaseproof paper as well.
3   Melt margarine and syrup, then stir in chocolate powder and remaining ingredients.
4   Press mixture down into the baking tray and put in the fridge to set – overnight.
5   In the morning, turn out onto a chopping board and cut into pieces for your consumption.

Very rich – freezes well.

I stopped doing this recipe a few years ago as it is not really 'healthy' and it panders to chocoholics. My staff ate more of it than anyone else!

Wholemeal Scones

1 lb wholemeal flour
2 oz margarine
1 tsp bicarbonate of soda
1 tsp cream of tartar
¼ tsp salt
½ pt milk

Method

1   Rub fat into flour and then add all other dry ingredients.
2   When the mix is like fine breadcrumbs, make a well in the centre and pour milk into this well. Stir in thoroughly.
3   Knead until pliable.
4   Roll out to ¾" thick and cut with a 2" plain scone cutter.
5   Place on a floured baking tray and bake at 200°C. for 10–15 minutes until the scones are risen and thoroughly cooked inside.
6   Cool on rack.

This is a firm favourite with health-conscious people. An acquired taste as it is nothing like ordinary white scones. We have converted many people over the years to these scones.

I have added dates, walnuts, cherries, sultanas, cheese – all sorts of ingredients over the years. The basic one is what I usually make as it can adapt to cheese, butter or jam and cream.

Chris's Pizza

Batch of scone mix – rolled out to ½", whatever shape you want.
1 400g tin chopped tomatoes
Pinch of basil or oregano
Grated mature cheddar cheese

Method

1   Cook pizza base. I prefer to cook one thicker base and cut in half length ways.
2   Top bases with grated cheese, spread tomatoes over the cheese and sprinkle with herbs. Top with more cheese.
3   Put on a baking tray and bake in a hot oven or grill until bubbling and golden.

If you are making this, you can add anything – ham, tuna, olives, peppers, mushrooms etc. I have always kept it very simple for the café.

Children can't cope with this base and just eat the top. But my staff (youngsters) just love it.

Wholemeal Pastry

4 oz wholemeal flour
1 oz vegetable margarine
1 oz Trex or similar
1 tsp baking powder
Pinch of salt
3–4 tbs cold water
1 tbs oil

Method

1   Put flour, baking powder and salt into a bowl or processor bowl.
2   Chop fats finely and rub/process into the above mix.
3   When the mix resembles fine breadcrumbs, add water and oil – enough to gather all the mixture together. Knead well.
4   Turn onto a floured board and use as required.

I use for quiches, fruit pies, savoury, and vegetarian dishes.

So much more flavoursome than 'white pastry' and so much better for you. I don't know why more places don't use it! There is an art to it I'm told. It is easy to use too much or too little liquid – it is a very fine balancing act. Practice makes perfect!

Crumble Mix

4 oz sunflower margarine
1 tbs millet
1 tbs sesame seeds
1 tbs linseeds
1 tbs desiccated coconut
1 tbs chopped mixed nuts
1 tbs oatmeal
1 tbs oat bran
2 tbs porridge oats
2 tbs soya or rye or maize flour

Method
1   Rub fat into all the above ingredients.
2   Sprinkle over the top of seasonal fruit in a dish.
3   Bake at 190°C until fruit is cooked and crumble is golden.

This mix can be adapted with more or less fat and minus any of the above, according to your personal taste. It is so tasty, healthy and easy – no wheat flour, no sugar. It really is a delicious topping that has been so popular over the years. It tops all our freshly picked fruits – gooseberries, raspberries, blackcurrants, rhubarb and date, damsons, apples, depending on the season. This can also be used for savoury crumble dishes.

Seville Marmalade

3 lb Seville oranges
6 lb sugar
3 lemons
1 ½ pints water

Method

Put clean jars in the oven to sterilise (190°C) for 10 minutes.
1   Wash and scrub the fruit.
2   Halve the fruit and squeeze out the juice from each half.
3   Gather all the pips into a muslin bag and put into a jam kettle or pressure cooker.
4   Quarter all the squeezed out fruit and add to the kettle with ¾ pint water and cook for approximately 30–40 minutes to soften the fruit. If pressure cooking, this will take about 10 minutes. Cool the mixture.
5   Lift out and squeeze the pip bag – discard.
6   Put the mixture into a processor and chop finely.
7   Put the mixture back into the pan, add the sugar and the remaining water.
8   Stir, bring to the boil slowly and stir until setting point is reached – when 1 tbs of marmalade will wrinkle when put onto a cold saucer.
9   Remove the jars from the oven and pour in the hot marmalade – carefully!
10 Put on the lid, label and store.

This is always popular on toast – it really does taste of oranges and is not over sweet. I do sell it to 'special customers', but usually end up giving it away to lots of friends as 'thank-you' presents.

Mulled Wine

1 bottle of red wine
8 oz dark muscovado sugar
2 sticks cinnamon
1 lemon
1 orange
8 cloves
1 pint water

Method
1   Thinly slice the orange and lemon.
2   Bring the water and the sugar to the boil, then add the spices and slices of fruit and continue to heat for 8 minutes. Then let it stand for 10 minutes.
3   Add the wine and heat gently for 10 minutes – don't boil.
4   Strain out the spices and the fruit.
5   Serve in warmed glasses with a fresh slice of orange and lemon.

This can be stored in bottles and reheated when required.

This is made each Christmas at Acorn for special customers and friends – always popular and the wonderful smell adds a festive touch.

Cakes

It has been a difficult exercise to decide, out of all the cakes I bake, which ten to include in this book. I have chosen some very popular ones that have various reasons for their popularity. Date slices are popular because they have no added sugar, flapjacks because they are not the dreadful sticky sweet ones you so often get.

The healthy fruit loaf is unusual because there is no added sugar and I have adapted it to have no wheat flour as well. Shropshire tea bread and Bara Brith are so quick, tasty and easy to make. They were a good use of our surplus tea and have always been very popular. Parkin evokes a very nostalgic memory of childhood and bonfire night. It's 'sticky and comforting', keeps well and again I have adapted it to include no wheat flour.

My carrot cake is the 'mother of all carrot cakes' I have never tasted a better one and this is backed up by numerous customers. The honey and ginger cake is lovely and light, moist and with lovely crunchy stem ginger. It is also included as a tribute to my godmother, Margaret, who was a wonderful cook and originally gave me the recipe.

Banana Malt loaf is great for using up over-ripe bananas and it is lovely and moist and tasty.

Apricot Slice

1 lb sunflower margarine
5 oz Demerara sugar
12 oz wholemeal flour
2 tsp baking powder
12 oz rolled oats
12 oz dried apricots, soaked overnight

Method

1   Drain apricots.
2   Heat oven to 180°C.
3   Grease baking tray (12"x 8").
4   Cream fat and sugar, add oats, flour and baking powder.
5   Spread half the mixture on the base of the baking tray, top with apricots, then top this with the rest of the mixture.
6   Bake for 30 minutes until golden and cooked.
7   When cool, cut into pieces and remove from tin.

Flapjacks

12 oz hard margarine or butter
10 oz golden syrup
10 oz dark Muscovado sugar
1 lb 12 oz – 2 lb rolled oats, jumbo or mixed

Method

1   Melt margarine or butter with sugar and syrup, stir.
2   When melted, add oats and mix thoroughly to form a firm, non-syrupy mix.
3   Grease a 12" square baking tin and press mixture firmly into tin.
4   Bake at 180°C for 30–40 minutes until golden and firm.
5   When still warm, cut but leave in tin until thoroughly cold. Remove and store in tins.

A flapjack that doesn't stick to the roof of your mouth and isn't too sweet and sickly!

Healthy Fruit Loaf

2 cups chopped dates
2 cups sultanas
2 cups raisins
1 cup cherries (natural)
4 cups gluten-free flour
2 tsp gluten-free baking powder
½ cup ground almonds
2 egg whites
2 tsp ground cinnamon
2 tsp mixed spice
2 cups soya milk
2 cups pineapple juice

Method
1   Put all fruit and spices in saucepan with pineapple juice and simmer for 3 minutes. Leave to cool.
2   Stir in remaining ingredients except gluten-free flour, which you finally fold into mixture.
3   Grease loaf tins – 3 small or 2 large.
4   Line with baking paper.
5   Bake at 170°C for 45 minutes – 1 hour, until a skewer inserted in to the centre, comes out clean.

No added sugar and gluten-free.

Date Slices

1 lb 2 oz sunflower margarine
¾ lb rolled oats
1 lb 4 oz wholemeal flour
3 tsp baking powder
3 tsp ground cinnamon
1 lb 8 oz chopped dates – soaked overnight

Method
1   Drain dates.
2   Cream margarine, add all other ingredients and mix thoroughly.
3   Grease a 12" square baking tin.
4   Line tin with half of the oaty mixture, spread drained dates on top and then top with remaining oaty mixture.
5   Bake at 180°C for 30–40 minutes.
6   Cool and slice. Remove when completely cold.

Moist Carrot Cake

12 fluid oz sunflower oil
12 oz dark Muscovado sugar
3 large eggs
10 oz wholemeal flour
3 tsp baking powder
1 tsp ground cinnamon
1 tsp mixed spice
1 tsp vanilla essence
8 oz grated carrot
3 oz walnut pieces
½ of 435g tin of crushed pineapple

Icing
200g soft cream cheese
1 oz icing sugar
Lemon juice to taste

Method

1   Whisk sunflower oil, sugar, eggs and vanilla essence.
2   Stir in carrots, pineapple and walnuts, then fold in dry ingredients.
3   Grease two large sandwich tins. Fill with mixture.
4   Bake at 180°C for 30–40 minutes. until the mixture is spongy and bounces back when pressed. Leave in the tins until completely cold. Carefully remove from tins.
5   To make the icing, cream creamed cheese, add sugar and lemon juice to taste.
6   Halve the icing, then when cool spread this half on bottom layer. Add top layer of cake, then spread remaining icing on top. Place a few walnut halves on top to decorate.

This cake is truly to die for!

Shropshire Tea Bread

1 lb currants, raisins and sultanas
1 egg
1 lb wholemeal flour
2 tsp baking powder
5 oz dark Muscovado sugar
1 pint cold tea (no tea leaves!)

Method

1   Soak fruit overnight in tea.
2   Mix all the ingredients together.
3   Grease loaf tins, line and then add the tea bread mixture.
4   Bake at 180°C for 45 minutes – 1 hour. When cooked, a skewer inserted in the centre comes out clean.
5   Leave to cool. Then remove from tins.

One of Acorn's favourite cake recipes. So quick, so tasty and uses up left-over tea! Usually served with butter, but doesn't need it as it is so moist.

Bara Brith (Welsh tea bread)

1 lb sultanas
1 lb wholemeal flour
4 oz dark muscovado sugar
2 eggs
1 pint tea
1 tsp mixed spice
1 tsp baking powder

Method
1   Soak sultanas and sugar in tea overnight.
2   Mix remaining ingredients together and add to the above.
3   Put into greased, lined loaf tins.
4   Bake at 170°C–180°C for 45 minutes until a skewer inserted comes out clean. Turn out when cool.
5   Serve with butter if desired.

This recipe was originally given to me by one of the vets' wives in West Wales when I was a representative of veterinary supplies. I have adapted it to wholemeal flour and it's been a firm favourite at Acorn since I opened.

I also do the above with gluten-free flour and baking powder and it makes a lovely gluten-free cake!

Parkin

½ lb hard margarine
½ lb dark Muscovado sugar
½ lb oatmeal, medium
¾ lb dark treacle
¼ lb golden syrup
½ lb rye flour
2 eggs
2 tsp ground ginger
2 tsp mixed spice
2 tsp baking powder
½ pint milk

Method

1   Melt margarine, syrup, treacle and sugar.
2   Cool, then add milk and eggs. Mix thoroughly.
3   Fold in all dry ingredients.
4   Bake in greased, deep tin – roasting type 8"x10" – at 170°C for 40–55 minutes. When springy to touch, it will be thoroughly cooked.
5   When cool, cut into squares and keep in an air tight tin. Improves and goes stickier when kept.

This is another recipe I've adapted for wheat-free customers and it's very popular.

Banana Malt Loaf

One third of a 370g jar of malt extract
2 oz margarine
1 lb wholemeal flour
6 oz sultanas
4 mashed bananas
4 oz dark muscovado sugar
½ pint milk
3 tsp baking powder

Method

1   Put malt extract into saucepan and melt with margarine, sugar and milk.
2   Fold in mashed bananas, flour, baking powder and sultanas.
3   Grease and line 2 large loaf tins or 3 small ones. If too stiff, add more milk. Spoon mixture into tins.
4   Bake at 170°C for 50 minutes – 1 hour until a skewer inserted in the middle comes out clean.
5   Turn out of tins when cool.

Serve buttered with a cup of tea for your afternoon break!

Honey and Ginger Cake

1 ½ cups honey
1 ½ cups sunflower oil
1 ½ cups cold tea
1 ½ cups dark Muscovado sugar
4 ½ cups wholemeal flour
Small jar stem ginger, chopped up
150g ground almonds
5 eggs
1 ½ tsp bicarbonate of soda
1 ½ tsp ground ginger

Method

1   Grease and flour 8"x10" baking dish (deep one).
2   Whisk egg whites.
3   Whisk all other fluid ingredients.
4   Then fold in egg whites and dry ingredients.
5   Pour into baking tin and bake at 160°C for 1–1¼ hours until spongy to the touch.
6   Cut into squares when cold and remove from tin.

Given to me by my dear, now departed godmother, who was always trying to convert people to her recipes. This really is delicious, lovely and moist and gingery (I added stem ginger).

It's a New Zealand recipe – hence the cup measures! A strange Kiwi thing.

Lightning Source UK Ltd.
Milton Keynes UK
UKOW02f0807241115

263366UK00002B/15/P